From
MADAGASCAR
to the
MALAGASY
REPUBLIC

From
MADAGASCAR
to the
MALAGASY
REPUBLIC

Raymond K. Kent

FREDERICK A. PRAEGER, *Publisher*

New York

BOOKS THAT MATTER

Published in the United States of America in 1962 by
Frederick A. Praeger, Inc., Publisher
64 University Place, New York 3, N. Y.

© 1962 by Frederick A. Praeger, Inc.
Library of Congress Catalog Card Number: 62-11772

Manufactured in the United States of America

Contents

To L. GRAY COWAN

Introduction

While not physically a part of Africa, from which it is
separated by the Mozambique Channel, Madagascar is
the nearest phenomenon to what may be called an
Africa in miniature, with a similar history and similar
problems. It is also, in many respects, unique in its
part of the world. In 1947, when most of Africa did
not have articulate nationalist movements, Madagascar
suffered a revolt of enormous intensity, a revolt that
took the lives of more than 1 per cent of its population
and almost successfully challenged French control. Yet
today, the Malagasy Republic is one of France's closest
allies. Similarly, at a time when some of the most astute
African leaders argue that the institution of opposition
parties cannot be expected to function in newly
emergent countries, Madagascar offers convincing proof
that such is not necessarily the case. While it does not
give new answers to the question of the desirability of
multiparty systems, Madagascar helps clarify what
makes a multiparty system possible in the important
initial stages of independence. Madagascar is also the
only area of tropical Africa in which a Communist-led
party takes part in the body politic. The Malagasy
experience with that party demonstrates not only *how*,

but what is infinitely more important, *why* it came into being.

In spite of its more than casual importance to Africa, and although a subject from which much can be learned, Madagascar has received scant attention in the English-speaking world. Aside from a few works of very limited interest and a scattering of articles in various periodicals, very little information about Madagascar is available to the English-speaking student. It is, therefore, the principal aim of this brief volume to bridge the gap until more detailed and more elaborate contributions will be made.

The field of African studies is being deluged with books ranging in approach from facile single-discipline scientism to journalistic superficiality, from ethnocentrism to questionable empathy and adulation, from total absence of scholarship to scholarship without intuition, from semantic complexity to oversimplification. It is the aim of this work to steer clear of those methodological pitfalls, to be simple, to worship no idols, to be sympathetic to both France *and* the Malagasy, to combine a certain amount of scholarship with intuition, and, above all, to avoid Lasswellian depths.

The transformation of Africa undoubtedly constitutes one of the most outstanding events of this century. But until very recently, the limelight focused on independence has diverted attention from other, equally important aspects of the great change. An even more unfortunate trend is the tendency to generalize from aberrations or from superficial analyses of those areas of the continent that are constantly in the headlines. As this study will attempt to show—in contrast to the headlines—Madagascar, affected by forces and ideas both within and outside the island, offers more than commonplace insights into the complex meaning of social change.

I

MADAGASCAR
AND THE MALAGASY

1

Notes, Problems, and Sources

Two years after Vasco da Gama's pioneering voyage to the Malabar coast of India, which indirectly led to the geographic and commercial discovery of Madagascar by Europe, a Portugese fleet led by Admiral Cabral was sent to explore the Indian Ocean on behalf of King Emanuel I. The discovery of these new trade routes dealt a heavy blow to the commerce and trade of the Middle East; centuries later, the opening of the Suez Canal was to deal a similar blow to Madagascan commerce.

Shortly after entering the waters of the Indian Ocean, the Portugese ran into a hurricane, and a ship commanded by Captain Diogo Diaz was separated from the fleet. On August 10, 1500, Diaz sighted a huge land mass hitherto unaccounted for on the map. He named it the Isle of St. Lawrence, after the patron saint of the day. As the French scholar Guillaume Grandidier put it, "And thus the existence of Madagascar was revealed to Europe by the caprice of the winds." [1] The next three centuries brought to Madagascar trading posts, missionaries and pirates, naturalists and agents of France, Holland, and England. Along with a modest sprinkling of Western civilization, the seeds of colonial-

3

ism were planted during these centuries, although no foreign power was to occupy the island until the end of the nineteenth century, when the age of great discoveries was replaced by the era of colonial expansion.

It is more than likely that the existence of Madagascar was known to both the Egyptians and the Phoenicians before the birth of Christ, but the first reliable reports concerning the "Great Isle" can be traced only to the tenth century A.D., and more specifically to the Arabs.[2] For example, Mas'udi, often called the Herodotus of the Arabs, visited both Zanzibar and Madagascar between 930 and 940 A.D. The Arabs did not know the island as "Madagascar." They called it "Djafouna" in the tenth century and "al-Qumar" (Isle of the Moon) in the eleventh. In his *Geographical Dictionary*, Yaqut (1179–1229), the greatest of Arab geographers, referred to Madagascar as "Waqwaq." * Although its origin remains unknown, it is in Marco Polo's account of his voyages that the appellation "Madeigascar" appears for the first time.† Thus a Venetian gave the island its lasting name, a Portuguese was the first European to discover Madagascar, while Arab historians and geographers furnished the earliest authentic reports about it. The Arabs found Madagascar inhabited; hence the question arises: Who were the original inhabitants, and how did they come there?

At one time Madagascar, it seems, had been a part

---

* Scholars are not in agreement as to whether Yaqut's island of *Waqwaq* was actually Madagascar or Japan. Gabriel Ferrand has concluded that there are two distinct *Waqwaqs*, Chinese and African—the first being Sumatra and the latter Madagascar. (See *"Le Wakwak est-il le Japon?"* *Journal Asiatique* [April, 1932], pp. 193–243.)

† *The Book of Ser Marco Polo the Venetian*, ed. Henry Yule (London, 1871), II, Book 3, chapt. 33, pp. 345–54.

of the continent of Africa, itself a part of the ancient Gondwanaland. Geologists have concluded that Madagascar became an island by being literally torn off by the same faulting force that created the great rift valley in the Middle East and Africa. Beginning with the question of whether or not all life on the island had been obliterated by the cataclysmic force of the split, there is a long list of improbable and contradictory as well as plausible theories dealing with the enigma of the original inhabitants. At least one source states that they were Bushmen who perished at the time of the split. Another goes even further and asserts that they managed to survive. Yet most of those who have devoted some study to the subject hold that there were no survivors, that the forefathers of the present-day Malagasy came by sea, and that they reached Madagascar at least a thousand years before the Christian Era.

Physically, the Malagasy are a highly mixed people, a complex of Negroid, Mongoloid, and Caucasoid types. According to George P. Murdock, "The Negroid element predominates, especially in the coastal regions, whereas the Mongoloid element is strongest on the interior plateau. The Caucasoid element, much the least significant, is most noticeable in . . . regions where there is definite historical evidence of Arab and European settlement." [3] Another authority, A. Rakoto-Ratsimamanga, notes that about 54 per cent of the population is Negroid, 32 per cent Indonesian-Mongoloid, and 9 per cent Indo-European. [4] The presence of the two pervasive ethnic types has led to two opposite schools of thought, one claiming that the first inhabitants came from nearby Africa, and the other holding that they came from one of the Indonesian islands. In a recent discussion of the problem, Murdock concludes that Borneo is the most likely home of the first Malagasy.[5] While there are tribes in which the Negroid type (Makoa) is predominant, as well as those in which the Indonesian-Mongoloid type (Merina) prevails, racial animosities as such are not a social and political issue of any real significance in Madagascar.* Whatever archaeological evidence may yet be found regarding the origin of the first settlers, it is infinitely more important to keep in mind that the present-day Malagasy cannot neatly be grouped along racial lines.

Madagascar is the fourth-largest island in the world. Located about 250 miles off the southeast coast of Africa, it stretches lengthwise almost 1,000 miles between the twelfth and the twenty-sixth parallels, covering an area of 228,000 square miles. Madagascar can be divided in three ways. In terms of topography, a broad division exists between the central plateau, which runs from north to south almost through the entire length of the island, and the coastal regions. This division plays an important role in the political history of Madagascar. Geologically, there are also two main parts: the higher crystalline massif, which covers about three fourths of the total area, and the lower western part, composed of sedimentary rocks.[6] Another division can be made by

---

* There is only one event in recent Malagasy history that can be said to have had some racial overtones—the creation of the PADESM in 1946, a political party of "disinherited" Malagasy most of whose membership seems to have had a somewhat darker complexion than the Merina. Thus, on August 1, 1946, *Voromahery*, the party paper, wrote: "We, too, are human beings. Our physical features may perhaps be less refined, our intelligence less perceptive, our nature more timid and self-effacing—but we are still human beings. We, too, are human beings capable of study, of acquiring a skill, of understanding science; capable of foresight and sacrifice, of serious and profound work."

so-called natural regions. The east is a humid mountain area with forested slopes and a narrow coastal plain. The Alaotra-Mangoro depression in the northeast is covered with trees and bush (*savoka*). The central plateau is largely a lateritic, grass-covered area, with the most temperate climate in the island. The west has gently rolling plains and is covered with grass and scattered woods. The Sambirano Valley region in the northwest is surrounded by forested mountains. The north, too, is mountainous, with forest and steppe cover; the south has very little tree growth and is covered with scrub.[7] Until recently, this last division has been of interest primarily to students of the island's general composition. During the last decade, however, it has tended to coincide with seven development zones under a joint Franco-Malagasy plan designed to improve the local economy.

The average annual rainfall for the entire island amounts to 25–30 inches, but it is by no means uniform. The south and the southwest receive slightly under 15 inches a year, while the eastern slopes and the adjacent coast get as much as 100 inches. Between these two extremes, the central plateau has an average yearly rainfall of 60 inches, while the northwest is only slightly more fortunate than the arid and semiarid south, with a brief but heavy rainfall in midsummer.[8] Although some excellent regional studies have been made since 1945, and more are scheduled to be completed in the near future, there is as yet no authoritative island-wide study of the soil. However, because much of the surface of Madagascar is covered with laterite, soil fertility is on the whole not very high.

Madagascar has a population of approximately 5

million. A division of this number by the total area of the island would yield an average population density of nearly twenty-two inhabitants per square mile. But the figure thus arrived at is a deceptive one, as will be seen from the discussion of recent internal migration and its significance. Considering the extent of Madagascar's coastline, the island, like Africa, is not very fortunate with regard to ports. There are eighteen ports, of which fourteen participate in international trade. Of these, however, the port of Tamatave alone accounts for 55 per cent of total international trade, while Tuléar, Majunga, Diego-Suarez, Fort-Dauphin, and Manakara account for an additional 32 per cent.[9] Moreover, the island's finest natural port, Diego-Suarez, is used relatively little because of its unfortunate location at the extreme north, away from the main shipping lanes, while the port of Tamatave is of poor quality and heavily congested.

An adequate discussion of the Malagasy people in their contemporary setting would require several volumes, and the undertaking would not be without considerable difficulties. Few peoples of Africa can claim as rich a body of literature about themselves as can the Malagasy, but the bulk of the work dealing specifically with the seventeen tribes that represent about 97 per cent of Madagascar's total population was written before 1939.[10] While the value of dated tribal literature cannot be disputed, and while the gap between today and yesterday is being slowly reduced by painstaking French and Malagasy scholarship,[11] much of the postwar discussion shows a preoccupation with "centrifugal forces" in Malagasy society. Such factors as tribal differences, traditional intertribal animosities, economic autarchy, and the lack of communications are cited, all based on research done from thirty to one hundred years ago.

The Antandroy, who live in the arid south of Madagascar have been consistently singled out as one of the island's most "backward" tribes. Thirty years ago, it is true, there were hardly any literate Antandroy, but today there are over 25,000. Moreover, during the last decade, significant advances have been made within the tribe as a result of the many new influences brought back home by young men who had left to work in towns and commercial establishments along the southeast coast. By comparison, the Merina have traditionally been regarded as the most advanced tribe in Madagascar. Admittedly, the vast majority of Malagasy intellectuals are Merina; in sheer numbers of doctors, writers, lawyers, artists, and poets (some of them with reputations extending beyond the island itself), no other group can compare with the Merina.* Nevertheless, there are many exceptions to this. Two of the leading intellectuals in Madagascar are not Merina; the President of the Republic is a Tsimihety; and in provinces other than Tananarive, the administrative personnel is recruited less and less from among the Merina (in 1958, only 60 per cent were Merina). In terms of social stratification, the Merina are still at-

* The best-known poets, J.-J. Rabéarivelo and Flavien Ranairo; sculptors and painters like Rasolomanitra, Razanamaniraka, and Randriamampito; scholars like Dr. Andriamanana, Razafintsalama, and A.-R. Ratsimamanga; as well as scores of others are of Merina parentage, at least on one side. Rabéarivelo's poem "The Flute Players" and Ranaivo's "The Water-Seekers" have been translated into English by Dorothy Blair from the original French (*African Voices*, ed. Peggy Rutherfoord [New York: The Vanguard Press, 1960]). Rabéarivelo committed suicide in 1937 at the age of thirty-six.

tached to the traditional patterns of nobility (*Andri-ana*), middle class (*Hova*), and descendants of former serfs (*Andevo*). But there is a growing number of Malagasy whose tribal affiliations are at best of secondary importance.*

Some of the tribes, like the Betsimisaraka, have been described as outgoing, friendly, and hospitable, while others, like the Sakalava, are said to be withdrawn, keeping mostly to themselves. Thus in 1952, two French historians wrote that "the dominant characteristic" of the Sakalava people was "distrust . . . extending even to close relatives," whereas they found the Betsimisaraka "timid, pleasant [and] very pliable." [12] To form lasting conclusions on the basis of these "natural" attitudes betrays a highly paternalistic outlook. For the fact is that the differences between a Merina and an Antandroy, or a Tsimihety and a Bara, are today far more pronounced in terms of functions and environmental conditioning than in terms of "natural" attitudes. A pastoral Bara does behave differently from a sedentary Tsimihety, and there are considerable differences between a Merina doctor and an Antandroy craftsman. As the sociologist Louis Molet has shown, individual outlooks tend to reflect the immediate environment.[13] Thus, for a Tsimihety the "world" is "good"; for a Merina it is "overwhelming"; and for an Antandroy it is "insolent and mirthful." The Tsimihety of today are one of the most dynamic Malagasy groups; the

* Because most of the intellectuals are Merina, the old division between the Merina and the rest of the Malagasy continues—if not in the minds of Merina intellectuals themselves and some non-Merina as well, it does exist, is felt, and is manifested by educated Malagasy belonging to groups other than the Merina. O. Mannoni's article *"La personalité malgache. Ébauche d'une analyse des structures," Revue de psychologie des peuples,* No. 3 (July, 1948), pp. 263–81, touches on this problem.

Merina are traditionbound; while the Antandroy provide a large part of the island's migratory labor force.

Also stressed in recent studies of the Malagasy tribes
are the so-called traditional animosities created through
earlier struggles for supremacy among conquest tribes,
as in the case of the Sakalava and Merina. In the mid-
eighteenth century, the Merina were a vassal state,
paying tribute to the Sakalava empires of Menabé and
Boina. Less than a hundred years later, the Sakalava in
turn became vassals of the great Imerina Kingdom. The
century of conflict did not end with Merina supremacy.
For reasons of self-interest, the Sakalava chiefs had,
during their period of ascendancy, received support
from France. Once the scales began to tip in favor of
the Merina, the Sakalava asked and obtained an alliance
that was later to become the basis for French claims to
Madagascar.* Although the Merina fought against
French possession of the island, they were openly
favored by the administration during most of the
French rule. This was in the nature of things, for the
Merina were not only the most numerous and "evolved"
people in Madagascar, but they also had an efficient
administrative system of their own, adapted to indirect
rule and of great value to the French. While, therefore,
the existence of intertribal tensions cannot be denied,

* Two "balance-of-power" situations existed. As Dandouau and
Chapus state: "With the authorization of De Hell, the Governor of
Bourbon, Captain Passot concluded a treaty in 1840 whereby . . . the
Sakalava chiefs abandoned to France all of their rights to the northwest coast from Ampasindava Bay to Cape St. Vincent." (*Op. cit.*, p. 26.)
The Sakalava-Merina rivalry also led the former to side with France
during the conquest period. One of the battalions with which General
Duchesne took Tananarive was made up mostly of Sakalava. The second balance-of-power aspect was the Merina policy of vacillating neutrality. The British and French were played off against each other with
varying degrees of success, until the fate of Madagascar was sealed by
an agreement between Great Britain and France.

the whole question needs to be qualified. Under any circumstances, the days of intertribal warfare are not likely to return, and it would be an error to judge the French presence in Madagascar solely on the merits of the use of patronage for perpetuating enmity among historically antagonistic groups. Finally, while traditional animosities have lost their impact, they continue to manifest themselves in subtle and nonviolent ways.

Still another frequently mentioned centrifugal factor is economic in nature. While conditions begged for the development of trade relations among neighboring tribes in many parts of Madagascar, only a few were able to attain economic symbiosis. One very plausible explanation for this is that most of the tribes deliberately refused to depend on this type of economy for reasons of security. In addition, the insularity and the vastness of Madagascar have produced effects regarded by many as adverse. Insularity has been said to have inhibited immigration, which an entire school of French economists and demographers had looked upon as highly desirable because depopulation had been one of the island's problems.[14] To develop the island's economy both in the agricultural and industrial sectors, a fairly large labor force is needed. Prior to the 1950's, the French stressed their belief that the labor problem would be resolved through a population increase estimated to add another 5 to 8 million inhabitants by 1970. Little consideration was given, however, to the availability of funds and capital, the ratio of those who work to those who would have to be supported, the very high probability that such a poulation increase (if correct) would boost the number of agricultural workers without a corresponding increase in farming efficiency or in industrial labor, etc. The thinking has changed, under the influence of United Nations studies on similar problems in other underdeveloped areas. The French became more concerned with greater agricultural efficiency rather than with a population increase as a better and sounder approach to the problem. Following some doctrinaire discussion among the Malagasy nationalists during 1958–59, there are indications that the Tsiranana Government has decided to devote major efforts to the agricultural sector.

Eighty per cent of the total area of Madagascar has a low population density—2.5 inhabitants per square mile—and the great size of the island had prevented the development of the economic exchange deemed necessary in view of the highly diverse regional agriculture. Lastly, poor communications have been considered as contributing greatly to the situation. Primary roads are scarce, and, with the exception of Tananarive-Majunga, Ambilobé–Diego-Suarez, and Tananarive-Brickaville, the network is confined to the central regions between Tananarive and Fianarantsoa, where an exchange economy has flourished for some time. Floods and heavy rains have tended further to reduce internal communications along some 16,000 miles of primary and secondary roads. And the 530 miles of railroad tracks duplicate some of the primary roads, with the exception of the Tolongoina-Fianarantsoa and Anivorano-Moramanga lines.

The economic picture of Madagascar has, however, changed considerably during the last decade. In 1953, the total population of Madagascar was 4,463,841. Three years later it rose by 313,384. Since 1957, the annual population growth has exceeded 200,000. This growth is also reflected in the increasing food consumption and a corresponding decrease in exports. Immigration is no longer considered an asset.

TABLE 1

BREAKDOWN BY POPULATION GROUPS
1956 AND 1958

Groups	1956 *	1958 †
Merina	1,128,293	1,248,531
Betsimisaraka	699,097	773,104
Betsileo	562,577	637,661
Tsimihety	343,717	363,897
Sakalava ⎫	338,492	316,212
Makoa ⎭		58,934
Antaisaka	279,968	302,354
Antandroy	278,423	277,144
Tanala	206,972	215,639
Bara	206,625	215,026
Antaimoro	163,633	178,215
Antanosy	130,894	148,132
Sihanaka	93,880	107,133
Mahafaly	78,470	78,398
Antanakarana	29,075	35,556
Antaifasy ⎫	44,546	28,453
Antambahoaka ⎭		17,723
Bezonozano	28,919	32,540
Comoreans	44,576	46,601
St. Marianeans	10,826	12,859
Indians ⎫	24,763	13,353
Chinese ⎭		8,039
French	66,089	68,430
Other	17,390	7,151
Total	4,777,225	5,191,085

* *"Recensements de la population," Bulletin de Madagascar,* No. 135 (August, 1957), pp. 658–59.

† *"Repartition de la population," ibid.,* No. 162 (November, 1959), p. 946, Table 2.

Another highly significant development is that of internal migration. In a recent work, Hubert Deschamps has shown to what degree internal migration has contributed to the breaking down of tribal barriers and economic autarchies as well as to the development of an exchange economy. Distinguishing between areas of permanent migratory settlement and of reversible immigration, he notes distinct gains in the growth of money economy, knowledge and application of better farming techniques, cultivation of new areas, and lessening of rigid tribalism. Thus he finds "the influence of migratory workers who return home has been the greatest in the more archaic [tribal] societies," while stating that "at least three fourths of Madagascar owes its economic life to the internal migrations." Lastly, he predicts that "it is largely through internal migrations that the Malagasy Republic will attain progress and national unity." [15] Similarly, there has been an increase in road building, coastal sea transport *(cabotage)*, and, above all, in airfreight transport. According to William A. Hance, "Madagascar has a surprisingly well-developed air-transportation system. With more than 400 airfields and emergency landing strips, of which 58 are served by scheduled flights, it has the densest airline net in the whole French overseas realm." [16]

The postwar discussion of Malagasy society has also tended by and large to overlook the forces making for cohesion. Here, insularity and a small population are not the only factors. Ancestor worship based on the immortality of the soul is prevalent among the Christian, Muslim, and "pagan" populations alike. To most of the Malagasy, the village is the center of social and

Groups	Tananarive	Fianarantsoa
Antaifasy	129	23,137
Antaimoro	1,022	130,758
Antaisaka	867	224,085
Antambahoaka	28	13,640
Antandroy	3,438	4,123
Antanakarana	3	3
Antanosy	360	990
Bara	2,756	86,342
Betsileo	28,184	505,512
Betsimisaraka	2,457	105,428
Bezonozano	442	46
Merina	1,076,038	40,498
Mahafaly	96	161
Makoa	641	70
Sakalava	3,195	197
Sihanaka	716	56
Tanala	396	198,461
Tsimihety	247	83
Other Malagasy	173	1,150
French Citizens	6,731	505
Native-born French	24,962	4,428
Other Europeans	1,723	259
Comoro Islanders	859	154
St. Marianeans	6	10
Chinese	1,285	1,602
Indians	2,177	602
Other Asiatics	63	38
Total	1,160,322	1,342,750

GROUPS AND PROVINCES (1958 CENSUS)

Majunga	Diego-Suarez	Tamatave	Tuléar	Total
1,540	894	986	1,767	28,453
18,939	19,998	5,262	2,236	178,215
22,914	10,173	5,394	38,921	302,354
127	137	3,766	25	17,723
10,318	12,888	8,057	238,320	277,144
201	35,347	2	—	35,556
1,867	1,759	1,478	141,678	148,132
10,532	1,337	961	113,098	215,026
51,792	8,524	5,561	38,088	637,661
17,919	81,521	565,109	670	773,104
1,960	154	29,933	5	32,540
55,890	12,892	48,981	14,232	1,248,531
1,100	1,584	177	75,280	78,398
38,460	13,672	1,979	4,112	58,934
104,211	56,673	250	151,686	316,212
25,508	1,352	79,494	7	107,133
2,581	1,816	189	12,196	215,639
242,071	101,106	20,358	32	363,897
108	644	231	349	2,655
2,759	1,648	1,821	1,179	16,383
3,188	5,302	10,959	3,208	52,047
570	392	466	333	3,743
27,862	14,701	1,520	1,505	46,601
91	909	11,841	2	12,859
680	1,540	2,754	178	8,039
3,626	2,018	1,067	3,863	13,353
19	562	38	33	753
646,833	389,543	808,634	843,003	5,191,085

economic life, and the family the principal social unit in which hierarchy is patterned in accordance with age, sex, and division of labor. The lingua franca, Malagasy *(Malgache)*, spoken in a number of minor dialects, also contributes to cohesion.* Indeed, in vast, diverse, and yet cohesive Madagascar, the intermingling of tribes, races, and cultures, the existence of a language understood by all and a subreligion practiced actively by an overwhelming majority—all these, plus the factors of insularity and small population—have led to the evolution of a social tolerance that is one of the keys to the present.

It would be difficult fully to describe the island of Madagascar without discussing the tribal peoples in some detail—a task far beyond the scope of this volume. Of necessity, therefore, short profiles are used here, which stress what is characteristic of each group rather than what is common to most Malagasy, although some of the common features will not be omitted. Except for a resumé of Sakalava-Merina precolonial rivalry, tribal histories are only alluded to—partly because much remains unknown, and partly because other traits of tribal societies as they are today seem to be of more immediate importance.[17]

---

* There "definitely is a unique Malagasy language, spoken by the entire indigenous population." For an excellent discussion of the language, see *"La Langue Malgache,"* in *Madagascar* (Paris: Cahiers Charles de Foucauld, 1950), pp. 211–22.

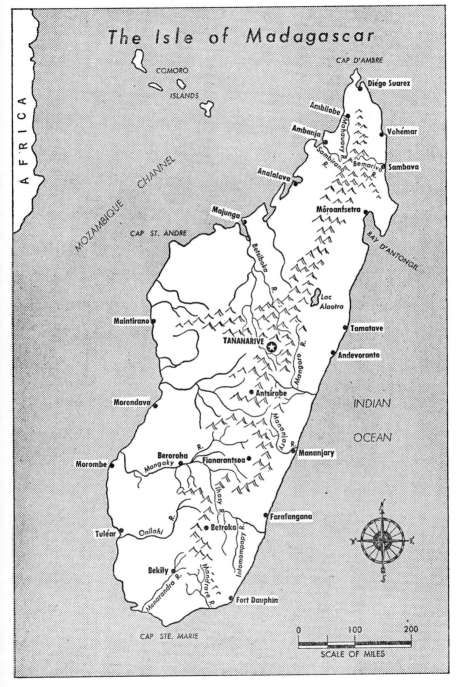

Geographic Map

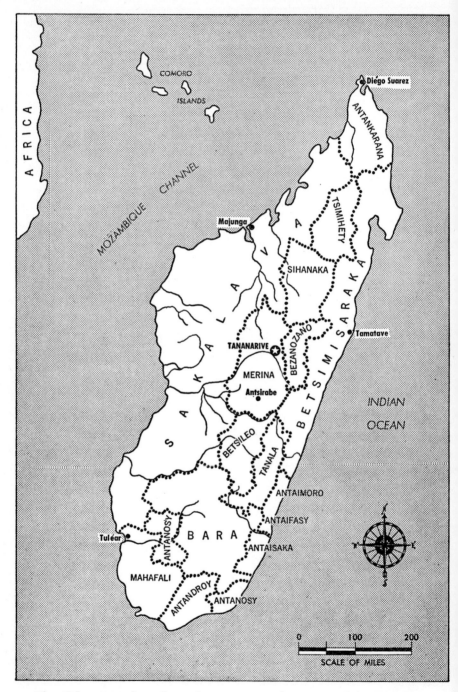

The Ethnography of Madagascar at the Turn of the Century

2

The Malagasy:
Portrait of a People

THE ANTANAKARANA

Dispersed mostly throughout the northern part of the island, the 35,000 Antanakarana live in what R. T. Batchelor once described as "without doubt one of the finest parts of Madagascar." Traveling in the north more than eighty years ago, he observed the "existence of wide rolling plains, which, being well watered and covered with good herbage, supply sustenance for vast numbers of cattle. . . . The country is also well wooded and the exportation of ebony and sandalwood from its central parts might, if properly managed, be the source of great wealth." [1] According to Batchelor, the Antanakarana, prior to being conquered by the Merina king Radama I (1810–28), were a united tribe, but split into two groups following a partially successful rebellion against the Merina. Those living on the west coast managed to preserve a great deal of independence, paying only a nominal poll tax once a year. The western Antanakarana had embraced Islam to some extent, though retaining their own marriage, domestic, and burial customs. The eastern Antanakarana were content to remain under the Merina rule and continued to resist Islamic influences. Today, the Antanakarana are mainly cattle raisers. Since the end of the last war, many of them have gone to work in Diego-Suarez and Vohémar, while others have sought work in meat canneries between Ambilobé and Diego-Suarez. Still others work seasonally on several east-coast plantations. The Antanakarana also grow corn, rice, and cassava.

Of the 30,000 residents in Diego-Suarez, some 3,500 are Antanakarana. No other city in Madagascar has as diverse a permanent population as does Diego-Suarez. Comoro Islanders account for some 20 per cent, French for 15 per cent, Sakalava for 12 per cent, Antanakarana for 11 per cent, Antandroy for 6 per cent, Merina for 5 per cent, and Malagasy from various southern tribes for another 5 per cent of its population. The remaining 26 per cent are made up of an assortment of Malagasy from central regions as well as Arabs from Yemen, Indians, Chinese, and Somalis. During the past fifteen years, Diego-Suarez has been the center of political extremism in the island. Among the rural Antanakarana, the historical split referred to by Batchelor has left a dual legacy. In some of the clans, the chiefs practice a modified form of Mohammedanism, while their followers remain firmly attached to the cult of the dead.* In others, the locus of power is to be found among the class of shamans, or wise men, whose origin traces back to an old priestly caste called "Onjatsy."

---

* The chiefs are said to be Khawaridj. The Kharidjites, once an important Islamic sect, survive only in Algeria, Zanzibar, and Oman. The northwest coast of Madagascar has been the main point of contact with Zanzibar.

THE SAKALAVA

South of the Antanakarana area, stretching along the west coast from Ampasindava Bay in the northwest, down to the Mangoky River in the southwest, is the traditional Sakalava country. The Sakalava, or "those who inhabit the long valley," are not a single, unified tribe, but a confederation of various independent clans. "There is no type that can be clearly depicted as Sakalava. . . . There are in fact several types that can be called Sakalava lacking a more precise name." [2] The Sakalava are predominantly Negroid. They are generally tall and well built. Those among them who have been partly Islamized still shave their heads and wear turbans. Among the independent clans grouped generally under "Sakalava," the Vezo and the Masikoro are the best known. Some 45,000 Vezo live in the vicinity of the port of Tuléar. They are excellent fishermen and seamen. A certain degree of economic symbiosis is in evidence between the Vezo fishermen and the Tanalana, an agricultural clan numbering several thousand. The Masikoro, some 60,000 strong, live near Morombé, Manja, Ankazoabo, and Tuléar. They were once a part of the Fiheranana Kingdom in the southwest. Together with the Bara, the Sakalava are the most pastoral of all Malagasy groups. "The Sakalava of today appears to be above all else a proprietor of cattle. . . . In most west-coast districts there are at least two, and often three, head of cattle per inhabitant." [3]

Many ancient customs have been preserved among the Sakalava. For example, they are probably the only group in the island still practicing trial by ordeal *(tsiripika)* as an ultimate test of justice. In spite of the inroads of modern medicine, diseases still tend to be "cured" through the sacrifice of a good bull or the *bilo*—a chanting prayer followed by verbal outbursts and a spasmodic, almost voodoolike type of dancing. Each family has its particular set of restrictive customs *(fady)* in addition to those of the clan and tribe *(lilindrazana)*. In contrast to a practice prevalent in many other Malagasy groups, some Sakalava chiefs retain considerable authority. This fact can be explained in part by the tradition of strong chiefs, dating back to the eighteenth-century kingdoms of Menabé and Boina, and in part by their position as both temporal and spiritual rulers.[4] During the colonial period, the Sakalava had often been described as highly conservative and introverted because "the economic development of the regions inhabited by them . . . far from providing the Sakalava with a sense of progress, was rather the cause for withdrawal. Not finding among the indigenous population a sufficiently developed and enterprising work force, the Europeans sought the help of workers from groups other than the Sakalava, the Merina in particular. . . ." [5] A more concrete proof of regression was furnished by the very low Sakalava birth rate, forecasting what may have been a trend toward extinction. This trend has been reversed as a result of the economic and cultural influences of immigrants from other tribes, particularly the dynamic Tsimihety.*

* The trend toward self-extinction is one of those rare, perplexing phenomena. A low birth rate in highly industrialized societies has been amply accounted for both in social and economic terms. The same cannot be said for tribal societies. In the case of Sakalava, economic factors explain the trend only to a degree. The feeling of "neglect" (translated to some extent in the 1946 political program of the Parti des Désherités Malgaches) contributes also to a fuller understanding. No French-language source has dealt authoritatively with the trend and with its reversal from the point of view of acculturation.

THE MAHAFALY

Farther south, between the Onilahy and Menarandra rivers, dwell the Mahafaly. Numbering close to 80,000, they live mostly in isolated villages surrounded by a maze of bush. Their huts are unusually small in size. In a Mahafaly family, the father is "king," while the women (who outnumber the men) are the real labor force. The children, too, are made to work at an early age. The men are still somewhat bellicose and continue occasionally to raid cattle herds in the Antandroy country. Since the 1930's, the relatively rigid tribal structure among the Mahafaly has been modified by economic changes. The introduction of new plants like cassava and rice and their diffusion, the presence of sisal plantations and processing plants, and emigration (mostly to Majunga and Diego-Suarez), as well as seasonal moving of livestock from one region to another and better conservation and use of meager water resources, have brought about new wants and new attitudes toward the traditional authority of the chief and the shaman.

Many Mahafaly still engage in idolatry and are attached to gold, although they do not seem to use it as a means of exchange. The Mahafaly are very gifted artists and an "aesthetic sense is apparent in their sculpture and wood carvings buttressed by [heavy] ornamentation." [6] "Their decorative style is reflected in the 'aloalo'—the long staffs . . . planted among rocks covering a tomb—carved in motifs possessing elegance." [7] The bulk of the Mahafaly live in the Ampanihy and Betioky districts. In the 1930's, there was a sudden interest in the preservation and revival of local arts and crafts. Scores of new ateliers appeared in the principal cities of the island, especially in Tananarive, and mohair rugs woven by the Mahafaly enjoyed particular success. Since then, the Mahalafy have developed a fairly lucrative rug-weaving and dyeing industry.

THE ANTANDROY

Separated from the Mahafaly by the Menarandra Valley, the Antandroy inhabit the southernmost tip of Madagascar. Tall and robust, the Antandroy are a pastoral people. Prior to the French occupation, cattle rustling was a widespread practice among them. It has not disappeared, although it is now practiced in a more covert manner.* Wealth among the Antandroy is measured in terms of the head of cattle in actual possession, and it is no different from wealth in any other society, measured in terms of purchasing power. (As recently as 1930, an Antandroy is reported to have committed suicide after the loss of his favorite bull.) The more cattle an Antandroy owns, the more wives he can get and the more children he can have; and the more children and wives, the larger his labor force and his feeling of security. The cattle may perish through disease or lack of water, or be stolen by a Mahafaly raiding party. But the labor force remains. The Antandroy grow fruit and vegetables in family gardens maintained exclusively by the women.

The Antandroy habitat is, as Hubert Deschamps has aptly said, draconic. The soil fertility is extremely poor,

* A recent law on cattle rustling (No. 388, 1958) provided for severe penalties, but it was amended in recognition of the fact that the stealing of cattle cannot automatically be regarded as a crime in regions where it has long been an accepted intratribal custom.

the climate extremely arid, and life harsh. Every few years, the Antandroy country seems to be invaded by locust swarms that destroy the fragile and carefully maintained farmlands. The Antandroy underwent three periods of famine—in 1930–31, 1936–37, and 1943–44, respectively—the last being the most severe. According to Charles Robequain, two Antandroy districts lost more than one third of their total population as a result of the last famine. In addition, one district reported the loss of some 50,000 head of cattle. The difficult environment, the famines and locusts, have contributed to heavy emigration to Tuléar as well as Diego-Suarez, Majunga, Tamatave, and, to a lesser extent, the Fianarantsoa and Tananarive provinces. Some 22 per cent of the Antandroy today are emigrants. Antandroy emigration dates back to the turn of the century. They are highly sought after. Their sense of pride does not permit them to lag behind in their work, and they obey authority (*fanjakana*) with relative ease. An accelerated exploitation of the neglected Sakoa coal mines and the possible emergence of an oil industry in the extreme south could change the pattern of migration. If successful, exploitation of large coal and recently discovered oil deposits would almost certainly affect the pastoral tribes of the south, including both the Antandroy and Mahafaly.[8]

THE BETSILEO

The Betsileo, the third most numerous group in Madagascar, live in the south in one of the island's highest plateau regions, bordered in the north by the Vakinankaratra Mountains, in the east by the Tanala tribe, and in the west by the Bara. They derive their livelihood from agriculture and are generally considered among the most skillful farmers of Madagascar. "The [Betsileo] rice * and garden cultivation, even on the steep slopes, is truly remarkable." [9] The Betsileo accord their old people a great deal of veneration. Except for the predominance of the Negroid type among the Betsileo, it may be said that they are perhaps closest to the Merina in customs, beliefs, and traditions. Both are said to have had common ancestors in the early Vazimba, and both were allegedly monotheistic prior to Christian influences. Their affinity with the Merina is also rooted in history. Sometime between 1750 and 1790, Andriamanalimbetany, King of the Isandra (one of the four great Betsileo clans), unified the Betsileo, bringing together under his rule the fiefs of Imanga, Lalangaina, and Vohibato as well as three lesser fiefs. According to Cheffaud and Dubois, his was a great and very prosperous kingdom. Following the death of this Betsileo monarch, the fiefdoms fought one another until Isandra and Lalangaina submitted voluntarily to Merina rule. Writing in 1877, G. A. Shaw reported as follows on the relations between the Merina and Betsileo:

> At the present time, the [Merina] Queen of Madagascar has placed governors at Fianarantsoa, Ambohimandroso, Imahozany, Ikalamavony, Ifanjakana, Imidongy and Ifenoarivo, each having a garrison of soldiers and ammunition. . . . Judges . . . are chosen by the Betsileo themselves. . . . The descendants of the old kings, called *anakandriana* or *anakova,* still retain a great deal of influence and authority in their separate spheres and are so

---

* Ralph Linton has given an excellent account on "Rice, a Malagasy Tradition," in *American Anthropologist,* No. 29, 1927, pp. 654–60.

recognized, *wisely*, by the present ruling government. They are now called *tompomenakely*, or lords of the manor, and are always ranked first in the *kabary* from the Queen. The Andevohova still retain their offices, being now however answerable [directly] to the government of Ranavalomanjaka and its representatives. It is . . . to be seen that although now in the position of the conquered, *the change has been one of vast improvement for the Betsileo. They have now peace and security, which they never had under their former government.* . . .[10]

The Betsileo have indeed been the favored subjects of the Merina kings and queens since approximately 1810, and shortly prior to the arrival of the French, the Merina were encouraging their Betsileo cousins to expand to the south, southwest, and southeast. French authorities have also fostered Betsileo migration throughout the island. The exceptional farming abilities of the migratory Betsileo have brought about increases in the production of rice and other crops to many areas of the isle. Moreover, the Betsileo emigrants included a high number of artisans, a factor that also had its impact by way of imitation. Until very recently, some 10–12 per cent of the 18,000 Malagasy public functionaries were Betsileo. Today, some 150,000 Betsileo live outside their home province of Fianarantsoa, most of them in the Majunga, Tuléar, and Tananarive provinces.

THE BARA

"Bara social units are composed of extended families called *Raza,* in which the descendants of common ancestors are grouped together. The members of any given *Raza* can be recognized by the way in which the ears of their cattle are marked, by [a uniform] family name, by adherence to [a given set of] taboos, and by the tradition of *Tatara-Raza,* or 'oral family history.' " [11] The Bara joint family is a patrilineal one and is perpetuated by exogamous marriage. Consanguineous marriage is considered incest, and thus taboo. Both the father and paternal uncles are called "father," while both nephews and sons are called "sons." The classification is not by age but by generation, and the entire *Raza* is ruled by the spirit of the original founder of the oldest generation, on whose behalf the local shaman-priest acts as the most respected intermediary between the living and the dead. Several *Raza* get together in village, or *Fuku,* which is then ruled by a priest acting for the generation that had founded the first *Fuku* by agreement (somewhat like the consensus among the leading pundits in Islamic Ijma'.) "The family group that founded the first village through agreement of all concerned often assures everyone—even a complete stranger—of a kind of magic protection." [12]

The role of the Bara chiefs seems rather ambiguous. They are honored, and until recently they supervised economic activities, leading an occasional cattle raid on other Bara clans (in this they differed from the Antandroy and Mahafaly, who seized cattle only from each other). But the real power is in the hands of the principal shaman-priest. The possession of cattle does not have only materialistic value, as among the Antandroy, where it is a means of securing a labor force. It goes beyond that, for a man able to create a *Raza* that founds a new *Fuku* will also become the ruling spirit. To create a *Raza,* one needs a great deal of cattle. This is a kind of

belief in predestination that compels one to be successful on earth, and while it has failed to create capitalism
among the Bara, in its own way it acts as a powerful
economic incentive.

There are five great clans among the Bara: the Bara-
bés in the valley of the Ihosy River, the Bara Imamono
in the vicinity of the Andazoabo township, the Bara
Iantsantsa near Ivohibé (which is connected by a fairly
good road to the port of Farafangana on the southeast
coast of Madagascar), the Bara Vinda in the vicinity of
the Onilahy River, and the Bara Antaivondro in the
high plateau area of the Intomampapy River. Until recently, the Bara tended to look upon agriculture as a
lowly occupation, but again migrations have modified
this outlook, and today there are quite a few Bara to be
found, for example, working as sharecroppers on the
tobacco plantations near Miandrivazo and Malaima-
bandy. The Betsileo influences from the north are asso-
ciated with a modest spread of agriculture in the Bara
country. There are roughly 113,000 Bara in the province of Tuléar, and about 86,000 in the province of
Fianarantsoa. The rest are to be found mostly in the
Majunga Province. The Bara are the most pastoral of
all the Malagasy. Robequain reports that in about 1940,
in the district of Benenitra, where considerable rice
cultivation is to be found, there were 17,300 head of
cattle, owned by 3,250 men, having a total value of over
4.5 million francs. At that time, a good bull could be
traded for as much as 1,800 lbs. of rice. The Bara also
grow cassava. Although social status among the Bara is
hereditary, the craft of shamanism is open to any Bara
child who shows promise.

THE ANTAISAKA, ANTAIMORO, ANTANOSY, ANTAIFASY, AND ANTAMBAHOAKA

These five southeast coast groups represent approximately one twelfth of the total Malagasy population. Administratively, they belong to the provinces of Fianarantsoa and Tuléar. The Antaimoro and the Antambahoaka have retained fairly strong Islamic influences. The Antaimoro have contributed some of the earliest known Malagasy-language inscriptions in Arabic letters, written in ink of their own making. The Islamized Antaimoro are limited to four noble clans, particularly the Antalaotra. The leaders of these noble clans trace their origin to Arab settlers who came to the rich and fertile Matitana Depression in the fifteenth century. Most of the Antambahoaka live in the Mananjary Valley. According to their oral traditions, all Antambahoaka derive from the same ancestor—King Raminia—who supposedly came from Mecca in the fourteenth century. The locus of power among the Antaimoro is neither in the hands of the chiefs nor of the shamans. It is to be found rather among the notables whose position (rank) is somewhat analogous to that of the Mu'tazila in the Arab world.* Although both the Antambahoaka and the Antaimoro have long since lost contact wtih the world of Islam, their noble clans resist alien intrusions, much as the Bosnian Muslims of Europe have done since the fall of the Ottoman Empire.

The Antanosy's original home is the region of Fort-

---

* The Mu'tazila used reason and analogy to interpret Islamic laws. The Antaimoro notables apply similar techniques to everyday problems, such as the settling of disputes.

Dauphin, site of the earliest French settlement in Madagascar. In 1830, the Antanosy came under effective Merina rule but rebelled ten years later, and Merina reprisals led to a mass movement of some 30,000 Antanosy into the Bara and Antandroy country. Subsequent migration toward the west increased the number of Antanosy emigrants to over 60,000. Thus about 40 per cent of the Antanosy live outside of their center of origin. The Antanosy were one of the last Malagasy groups to be pacified by the French. Recent economic gains in the region of the Mandrare Basin have arrested the westward movement of the Antanosy. The greatest concentration of the Antanosy is in the districts of Fort-Dauphin (55,000) and Betioky (40,000).

The Antaisaka, according to Deschamps, are a highly mixed group. Their noble clans, like the Rabehava and Zarafaniliha, came from the Mankogy area of the Sakalava territory, while the Antaisaka "commoners" are composed of Bara, Sakalava, and several other tribal aggregates. Finally, the "assimilated" clans, like the Antemanambondro confederation, are of Tanala descent. The diverse origins of the Antaisaka clans do not, as may be supposed, prevent the continuation of cohesive relationships rooted deeply in religious and social conformity—two agents that have tended to foster mediocrity and inactivity, from which the only possible form of escape is emigration. Thus, in Deschamps' words, "The cohesion of socal structure and the obligations toward the cult of the dead tend to contribute to the economic causes of emigration." While most Malagasy believe in the cult of the dead, not many are as conformist today as the Antaisaka, and fanatical devotion to that cult can be the cause of extreme economic hardships. Economists concerened with the island of Madagascar have noted time and again the extent to which funerals and long funeral feasts can deplete the economic resources of a Malagasy family, even those comparatively well to do. The practical manifestations of the cult of the dead tend to become less modest among the more archaic and rigid groups. Deschamps cites a report that the *kibori,* or tomb, of a recently buried Antaisaka leader cost about 850,000 francs CFA, plus fifteen sacrificial prime bulls, not to mention the additional costs of food and drink.

Within the Antaisaka clan, no one is allowed to earn cash—a practice that can be readily understood—but no one is allowed to work outside the clan for money, either. The only way to enrich oneself is to emigrate. Overpopulation has also been a constant factor in Antaisaka emigration. In many parts, the population density exceeds 100 persons per square kilometer and in some, even 200. Emigration has not been an unmixed blessing, however. Cassava, rice, and coffee production in the Antaisaka country has been sluggish, because most of the able-bodied and young tend to leave. The Antaisaka are among the principal purchasers of Bara cattle, most of it bought with money sent home by emigrants. In 1956, a single post office in Vangaidrano had delivered about 10 million francs CFA, by money orders, to local Antaisaka, a sum sent by relatives who had gone elsewhere.

Most of the 28,000 Antaifasy live in the vicinity of Farafangana. They came from continental Africa via the west coast and are engaged mostly in the cultivation of coffee.

THE BETSIMISARAKA

The Betsimisaraka occupy a sizable portion of the east coast, close to 400 miles in length and varying in width from 20 to 50 miles inland. In the north, their territory begins at the Bemarivo River, ending at the Mananjary River in the south. The principal city of their region is the port of Tamatave, with a population of about 45,000. With the exception of the year 1825, when they revolted against Merina hegemony, the Betsimisaraka have always accepted outside authority.* They are no longer the exceptionally able seamen known to have gone with their pirogues all around Cape d'Ambre to the Comoro Islands and back. James Sibree has given a description of one of these boats:

> I examined with interest the construction of the craft; it was about 30 feet long by 8 feet beam, and easily carried fifty people. The planks, about 8 inches broad, were *tied,* not nailed together, by twisted cord of anivona fiber, one of the toughest-known vegetable substances, the holes being plugged with hard wood. The seat boards came right through the sides, so as to stiffen the whole, for there were no ribs or framework. The seams were caulked with strips of bamboo, loops of which also formed the rowlocks for the large oars of European shape. The ends of the boat curved upwards considerably; and from its whole appearance it seemed likely to stand a heavy sea without danger. These boats are made for going to the shipping, for no canoe could live in the surf constantly rolling along these shores.[13]

* The overt acceptance of outside authority has often misled social scientists into believing that the Betsimisaraka lacked dynamism. Some of the most violent outbreaks during the revolt of 1947, however, occurred in Betsimisaraka districts.

Primarily of Negroid stock, the Betsimisaraka, numbering almost 800,000, are the second-largest group in
Madagascar. Today, they are to be found working in
graphite mines near Vatomandry and Brickaville; in the
vanilla districts of Antalaha, Andapa, and Sambava; in
the sugar-processing plants and port facilities of Tamatave; in cocoa and clove plantations; and in rice pad-
dies. As Robequain puts it, "The great [economic]
transformation among the Betsimisaraka reflects the
rapid indigenous adaptation to an export-oriented
economy. . . . Commercial cultivation has brought nothing but benefits to the Betsimisaraka. It has been the
source of cash income, often unexpectedly large." De-
tribalization seems to be taking place among the Betsimisaraka at a relatively rapid pace. "From Mahanoro,"
according to Deschamps, "as well as other rural areas
of the Betsimisaraka, young people flock to Tamatave,
hiring themselves out—the boys as employees and
drivers, the girls as domestic servants—often against
parental wishes, to see the 'new.' They return with new
and independent habits, and the parents accuse them
of frivolity, laziness, and bad temper." Translated
freely, a recent Betsimisaraka proverb quoted by Deschamps states: "Why go far when fortune waits at your
own doorstep?" The pertinence of this proverb lies in
the fact that the Betsimisaraka have become too concerned with cash crops, neglecting those not sold, but
consumed locally. "The Betsimisaraka has formed a
habit going back to the years of easy profit, whereby
he buys rice surplus from other regions of the island,
from [the] Alaotra [lake] or the central-plateau regions.
The profits are diminishing but the habit persists." [14]

Most of the Betsimisaraka migratory movements have
been in a northerly direction along the east coast. There

are about 50,000 members of the tribe in the three northern vanilla districts mentioned above. Another 18,000–20,000 are in Vohémar. The city of Tamatave is about evenly divided among the Betsimisaraka, Merina, and "all others"—each numbering about 15,000. The largest concentrations of Betsimisaraka are in the districts of Fénérive (130,000), Nosy-Varika (75,000), Tamatave (70,000), Mahanoro (70,000), Vatomandry (60,000), and Brickaville (50,000). The main unit among the Betsimisaraka is not the joint but the primary family, dominated by the father. The locus of power among the Betsimisaraka, if it can be pinpointed with any degree of accuracy, seems to be in the village councils.

THE SIHANAKA

The Sihanaka live around Lake Alaotra in the northeastern part of Madagascar. Their principal occupations are rice cultivation, fishing, and cattle raising. Prior to 1824, the Sihanaka successfully resisted Merina efforts to subjugate them. For seventy years after that date, until the arrival of the French, they remained under Merina rule. The five years preceding the transition from Merina to French rule were marked by a series of minor Sihanaka revolts. Sihanaka means literally "those who erred into the marshes." Actually, the movement of the Sihanaka into the Alaotra marshlands was quite deliberate, as they had sought to escape not only domination by the Merina but possible absorption by the Betsimisaraka.

The region of Lake Alaotra offers an interesting case study in colonial development. During the first two decades of the 1900's, attempts were made to grow various cash crops, such as tea and coffee, in ever-larger quantities. Irrigation and drainage projects were initiated during the administration of Governor Victor Augagneur (1905–10). None of these materialized, however. In fact, the production of rice increased after World War I, largely as the result of high market prices generated by immediate postwar demand. The preparation of rice beds, water saturation, transplanting, shallow plowing and digging, draining, hoeing, and reflooding, as well as reaping, binding, drying, grain removal, and storage—all continued to be done manually. Whenever more rice was needed, the Sihanaka would add a rice bed or two to the already existing ones. The few Europeans who owned rice fields used the *métayage,* or share-cropping, system with Sihanaka sharecroppers simply continuing the traditional manual methods of cultivation. Between 1919 and 1921, however, European interests were able to put through the first large-scale scheme involving the cultivation of cassava instead of rice. This was followed by the construction of several medium-sized plants for the processing of tapioca and rice. The timing of these developments was not accidental, for the Europeans knew that a railroad was being constructed to link the Alaotra region with Moramanga, and through it with the port of Tamatave. With the completion of the rail link in 1922, increasing numbers of Europeans came to settle in the region. Their interest was spurred not only by the new transportation facilities, but also by several surveys of the area by J. Longuefosse, a noted physical geographer, which stressed the unimpaired soil fertility and indicated in what direction future development of the area should be channeled. The unanimous verdict of Longuefosse and other experts was that the Alaotra region should become "the rice basket of the island." It took more than thirty years to develop this rice basket. Instead of improving the traditional methods of rice cultivation or of thinking in terms of development for the whole region, the European settlers merely superimposed small-scale commerce (usually one-family) and processing on what the Sihanaka could grow given a good rainy season. Most Europeans in the area became, in effect, intermediaries between the Sihanaka farmer and the commercial world. In 1937, for example, there were only a dozen out of 133 Europeans residing in the area who could be called farmers in the true sense of the word. As a rule, the Europeans believed that it was beneath their dignity personally to engage in riziculture. The few true farmers, without exception, grew cassava, a soil-tolerant crop. It was not until the 1940's that a slow advance on the rice-basket idea was made through better use of available fertilizers, rice amelioration (larger amounts of *Vary-lava,* a Carolina type of rice, were grown), limited but successful reclamation works, flood control, and the purchase of crop-processing machinery.* Finally, during the 1950's, the Sihanaka themselves began to reap increasing and long-overdue benefits from the exploitation of Alaotra.

There are today some 1,000 Europeans, 500 Chinese,

* The first display of a more positive attitude came in 1939, when J. Galland, long a foreman on one of the European-owned rice farms, decided to invest his savings in a farm. At first, he followed the Sihanaka method of cultivation using an improved plough. By 1941, Galland had a one-year rice reserve. He sold the excess, and, by adding what was left of his savings, he purchased a tractor, a pulverizer, and a leveling machine. By the end of 1943, Galland owned three sturdy buildings and an impressive mansion. It was not long before every settler in the area realized that if he, too, wished to own a villa he must do two things: shift to rice cultivation, and mechanize. In modernizing his farm, Galland had the advice and support of Georges Cours, an agricultural expert who, in 1931, became director of a highly respected institution in Madagascar: the Lake Alaotra Agricultural Station.

and 200 Indians in the Alaotra region. Administratively, the Sihanaka belong to the provinces of Tamatave (75,000) and Majunga (25,000). Ambatondrazaka, the home district of the Sihanaka, alone accounts for almost 99 per cent of the Sihanaka living in the Tamatave Province. Sihanaka emigration is almost negligible. Not more than a few hundred leave the region annually to work on vanilla and coffee plantations near the east coast.

THE BEZONOZANO

The Bezonozano are said to be an appendage of the Betsimisaraka and Sihanaka groups. The part of the island inhabited by them is called Ankay, and it is located in the valley of the Mangoro River, between a great forest and the central plateau. Lake Alaotra, the largest in Madagascar, marks their traditional northern boundary. The Tanala are to the south of them and the Merina to the west. The Bezonozano preserved their independence until the late eighteenth century. They had no strong chiefs. Called *mpifehy,* their chiefs were elected for limited periods of time and had no real authority. "The organization of this tribe was characterized by a kind of passive anarchy, the negation of all forms of authority." [15] The lack of a centralizing force, together with frequent internal strife among the clans, apparently paved the way for Merina conquest. For tax purposes, the Merina divided Ankay into eight administrative units. Taxes were rendered in the form of produce. From the early days of Merina hegemony, as well as throughout the first decade of direct French presence, the Bezonozano were a hard group to control.

The diffused nature of authority there, plus the fact that the Merina used Ankay as a kind of penal colony for nonconformists, gave the Bezonozano a reputation for individualism that has survived. The Bezonozano, a tall and handsome people, are predominantly Indo-Melanesian. Most of them live in the district of Moramanga (27,000), which they share with some 40,000 Betsimisaraka.

THE TSIMIHETY

In 1933, there were about 150,000 Tsimihety; today, there are more than 400,000. Not long ago they were considered to be merely an extension of the Sakalava. Now they are colonizing the former Sakalava territories around Majunga. Their stage of political development is that of the clan, of which there are more than forty. The largest among them are the Antandrona, Maronmena, and Maromainty. Cultivable areas are within clan jurisdiction but are owned by individual families. Cultivation is a collective endeavor involving extended families. The Tsimihety are one of the few Malagasy groups to have preserved their independence effectively during Merina supremacy. While the Merina occupied their territory in 1823, the Tsimihety allowed them to do so only at the cost of a treaty giving their own clans complete autonomy. Only the Merina garrisons at Mandritsara and Marotandrano remained as symbolic tokens of Merina hegemony. During the French conquest in 1895, the Tsimihety refused to fight, claiming that their participation in a war against France would go beyond the stipulations of the treaty concluded with a Merina king, Radama I. Subsequently, French control fared little better than had Merina control. In theory, the Tsimihety accepted French rule without protest. In practice, they continued to disregard all manner of foreign control. According to Pierre Launois, "The Tsimihety, fragmented in a multiplicity of clans isolated from one another by natural [geographic] boundaries, would unite at once to preserve their independence. . . . The village consists actually of a single [extended] family obeying the *Sojabé*—elderly men possessing both experience and prestige. . . . Today . . . new influences can be introduced among the Tsimihety only through persuasion of [local] dignitaries and village councils, not through the intervention of administrators representing the government." [16]

According to Deschamps, no other Malagasy group can compare with the Tsimihety in terms of mobility. Louis Molet has observed that it is only in exceptional cases that one will find an old Tsimihety born and buried in the same village who has not traveled a distance of at least 200 miles by foot. There are few Tsimihety to be found outside the northern part of the island. Their primary tendency is not emigration but expansion. There are close to 250,000 Tsimihety in the province of Majunga, another 100,000 in the province of Diego-Suarez, and some 20,000 in Tamatave Province. Molet explains the Tsimihety increase on the ground that, while they do not fear unknown risks or hard environment, they never travel beyond a point of no return—hence their slow and progressive expansion rather than sporadic but fairly massive emigration taking them far away from their original homes. The Tsimihety, a mixture of Negroid and Indo-Melanesian types, are of medium height. A considerable number of

Makoa have been integrated into the Tsimihety.* The Tsimihety remains primarily an agricultural worker. "The Tsimihety wage earner adapts himself to any type of weather and all manner of work: rice, vanilla, tobacco, coffee, yams, sugar cane, and raffia processing— even work in cities—but he rarely relinquishes his freedom by signing a contract, with the exception of those permitting him to become a sharecroper, which allows him a feeling of being his own master, working the good earth." [17]

THE TANALA

The name Tanala means "forest people," which is exactly what they are. Divided into two large subgroups, Tanala Menabé and Tanala Ikongo (so named after Mt. Ikongo), they live mostly within an area stretching southward from the Nosivola River to the valleys of Matitana and Ambahive at the southernmost end. The Tanala are skilled fishermen, using harpoons for their larger catch. One of the few people to collect wild honey, they use it for the making of intoxicating beverages as well as a substitute for sugar. Owing to the absence of cattle in their territory, the Tanala frequently hunt hedgehogs, lemurs, and birds to supplement their meager meat supply. Most of the Tanala engage in agriculture and, to some extent, in food gathering. In spite of frequent bans, the Tanala continue to follow the slash-and-burn method (*tavy*) of cultivation. Robequain notes that, in proportion to land under actual cultiva-

---

* Although the Makoa, over 50,000 strong, are today considered a Malagasy tribe, they are relatively recent arrivals, having come from Mozambique as slaves. It is indeed difficult to locate any district in which they represent more than 16 per cent of the local population.

tion, the *tavy* surface is by far greater among the Tanala landholdings than within any other traditionally tribal area in the island. While most Malagasy villagers engaged in rice cultivation keep their reserve supplies near their homes, the Tanala rice granaries (*homby*) are often to be found a day's journey from the village.

The known Tanala history has always been turbulent. Interclan strife did not end until one of the Antaimoro nobles, whose ancestors had fled in the sixteenth century from their own tribe and found refuge among the Tanala, founded the first Tanala kingdom, that of Ikongo.* Subsequently, the Tanala fought the Antaimoro with varying degrees of success—from the conquest of the Antaimoro stronghold of Vohipeno to retreat deep into their own region—until the establishment of Merina supremacy. Following the French pacification of the island, Tanala history appears less tragic only if compared to that of the Antandroy. But while the latter owed their misfortunes to a lack of water resources, to locusts and famines, most of the Tanala hardships were man-made. Thus some of the Tanala chiefs favoring the new administration used their new power to carry out reprisals against some of the clans that did not recognize their rule. After World War I, a harsh campaign was undertaken against the *tavy* practice in an attempt to preserve the dwindling forests in the Tanala country. In the first half of the 1920's, the Tanala were placed under an administrator born in the French West Indies who used great pressure to force them into the cultivation of coffee and raffia, in the belief that the only way to improve Tanala living stand-

* According to oral tradition, this king, Andriamatahitany, was both an astronomer and interpreter of sacred manuscripts written in Malagasy with Aabic letters.

ards was to impose "dynamism" from the top, using strong-arm measures, for the "good of the people." The Tanala were also pressed into railroad construction and into helping in the construction of the port of Tamatave during the first half of the 1930's.

Never adjusting well to outside authority, the Tanala seem to have been the only Malagasy group as such to have incurred the frequent wrath of the various successive administrations. Among the strongest supporters of the 1947 revolt, the Tanala were almost decimated by reprisals. They have since recovered and are advancing steadily under the influence of Bara, Antaimoro, and other immigrants from the south, as well as from the Betsileo in the northwest. Robequain states that there is a marked improvement in Tanala rice-cultivation techniques, and that under the impact of Ambaniandro, or "people from the highlands," new farming unions are being formed. The growth of agricultural unions may be due in part to the sense of teamwork, which the practice of *tavy* has fostered among the Tanala. It also reflects a favorable social structure. As is true of most Malagasy, "labor of production [among the Tanala] is . . . divided within the family by age and sex, and kinship so regulates . . . social interactions of members as to make the family a harmonious and efficient producing, distributing, and consuming unit." [18] Today, about 200,000 Tanala live in the Fianarantsoa Province and another 12,000 in the province of Tuléar. Their home districts are those of Ifandaina (55,000), Mananjary (50,000), Fort Carnot (35,000), Manakara (25,000), and Farafangana (15,000).

Before taking up the discussion of the Merina, the major Malagasy group, a brief historical digression

seems in order. In the early part of the fourteenth century, small feudal kingdoms were set up along the
coastal regions of Madagascar by chieftains of predominantly Arab stock. Several archaeological excavations
were carried out in Madagascar after World War I, and
at least one Arab town and many artifacts have been
uncovered in the vicinity of Vohémar. The archaeolo-
gists who discovered the ruins believe that the Arab
town was built in the late eleventh or early twelfth century. Arab influence on various aspects of Malagasy life
has been considerable along the coasts. The practice of
circumcision, the communal grain pool, various forms
of salutation, as well as the Malagasy names for seasons,
months, days, and coins, provide contemporary evidence
of Arabic influence.[19]

The period between the fourteenth and seventeenth
centuries also saw the establishment of various pirate
"republics" in Madagascar. In his *Histoire de Charles
XII*, Voltaire recalled that the "pirates of the European
and American seas were organized and were in Madagascar and its waters, making the last stand against the
lawful governments of the world." [20] For an extended
period, the pirates were not unpopular among the Malagasy. They provided the coastal populations with firearms and with clothing; showed them some improved
farming methods; gave them an example of a different
system of government with its unwritten laws, codes of
"honor," and equality of leader and followers; and introduced a number of new customs. The increase in the
slave trade brought the relatively amicable relationship
between the pirates and the coastal populations to an
end. "The continual preying on the tribes for slaves
provoked war with the natives, who turned against the
pirates the skill that the pirates had taught them." [21]

During the same period, Madagascar became a trading area for the French and British East India companies as well as for Dutch merchants. A number of trading outposts were established on the coast and in the interior of the island, and the entire era was marked by a kind of "open-door" situation. The seeds of colonial aspirations were planted along with the establishment of these trading outposts. As early as 1640, Walter Hamond, an English trader in Madagascar, wrote that "the inhabitants of the isle called Madagascar are the happiest people in the world . . . with most probable arguments of a hopeful and fit plantation of a colony there, in respect of the fruitfulness of the soyle, the benignity of the ayre, and the relieving of our English ships both to and from the East Indies." [22] Or, on the French side, *"L'an 1642, le sieur Rigault, capitaine de la marine, obtint de feu Monsigneur l'éminentissime cardinal duc de Richelieu, chef et surintendant de la marine, navigation et commerce de la France, pour lui et ses associés, la concession et privilège d'envoyer seuls, en l'isle de Madagascar . . . pour la y ériger colonies et commerce . . . au nom de sa Majesté très-chrétienne . . . laquelle concession fut confirmée par sa Majesté."* [23]

The first French settlers, who followed Rigault in 1643, were for the most part semimilitary personnel charged with the specific mission of forming a supply line in Madagascar to help France compete for India and the Mascarene Islands. They erected the first fortress on the island, Fort-Dauphin, and sought to rename the island "l'isle de Fort-Dauphin." The little French colony met with success for the next twenty-five years, and reputedly Franco-Malagasy relations reached the apex of harmony between 1643–53 under the leadership of Étienne de Flacourt. In 1654, De Flacourt was re-

placed by another *gouverneur* who acted as a petty ty-
rant, as did others that followed him. On Christmas
Eve of 1671, the entire French settlement and garrison
at Fort-Dauphin were massacred. Other settlements and
garrisons were subsequently established with more success, remaining mostly on the coast. The interior was,
on the other hand, penetrated by a new type of man who
was neither interested in making money nor in escaping
the "lawful" governments of the world. This was the
missionary, and from the nineteenth century to this
day, his role in the social and political life in Madagascar has been of great importance.

Whatever term may be used to denote the state of
affairs in the island before the eighteenth century, none
is more precise than "insecurity," in the group rather
than in the individual sense. According to Adolphe
Bruniquel, "All of the populations had to cope with a
state of intolerable anarchy." [24] One of the tribes that
tried to cope with the internal chaos was the Sakalava.
Toward the middle of the seventeenth century, a confederation of Sakalava clans started the great march
northward from the Fiheranana Valley, their original
home near Tuléar. Under the able leadership of Andriandahifotsy, a chieftain of Arab descent, the Sakalava,
possessing firearms as well as a paramilitary organization, moved across the Morondava region all the way
north to Majunga, which became a great trading center
by the middle of the eighteenth century. By the beginning of that century, the Sakalava had established two
fairly large kingdoms, those of Menabé and Boina (Bou-
éni), ruled by Andriandahifotsy's two sons, Andrama-
nanety and Andriamandisoarivo. The latter ruled
Boina.

[Andriamandisoarivo] died after reigning thirty years. His memory became the object of a real worship by the people; his name was honoured in all political and religious ceremonies, and his spirit invoked on all occasions touching the interests of the nation. At his death the kingdom of Iboina . . . reckoned among its tributaries the most important tribes of the island . . . including the Antandrona, the Bezonozano, the Sihanaka, the Manendy and the Hovas.[25]

At the peak of its power the kingdom of Menabé extended over most of southwestern Madagascar.

Another attempt to terminate intertribal and interclan wars—hence the condition of constant group insecurity—took place on the east coast during the seventeenth century in what is now Betsimisaraka territory. After decades of struggle, the Tsitambala confederation managed to subjugate the clans around Tamatave and Fénérive. In the eighteenth century, the harsh Tsitambala rule came to end, when, under the leadership of Ratsimilaho—son of an English pirate and a princess of the Zafindramisoa tribe—the subject peoples rebelled. Ratsimilaho, who had studied in England, founded Betsimisaraka, or the kingdom of the "many who are united," the first viable kingdom on the east coast. He made an alliance through marriage with the king of Boina and developed commerce and agriculture. Some historians consider Ratsimilaho to have been one of five most enlightened Malagasy rulers in precolonial history. He died in 1750.

Both the Sakalava and the Betsimisaraka kingdoms were short-lived. An inner struggle for power resulted in the formation of two shaky Sakalava states after the death of Andriandahifotsy's two sons. The Sakalava managed to regroup for several years under a much-respected queen, Ravahiny, a ruler of Boina admired even by Andrianampoinimerina, the greatest of all Merina conquerors. The twelve sons of Ravahiny soon brought back the state of insecurity, until the Merina stepped in by invitation. The death of Ravahiny, in 1808, marks the end of Sakalava power. The last of the Sakalava kings died in exile in Zanzibar. Similarly, on the east coast, interclan marriages led to new and contesting dynasties, which ultimately caused the disintegration of the Betsimisaraka Kingdom. Ratsimilaho's son was killed in 1767. His immediate successor, Iavy, held the clans together with a strong army for twenty-four years, but after his death, in 1791, the kingdom collapsed rapidly. The last Betsimisaraka king was killed in 1803 by his own subjects. One of those who contributed to the process of disintegration was Count Benyowsky, a Polish-Hungarian soldier of fortune who first proclaimed himself ruler of the Moroantsetera region of the Betsimisaraka Kingdom and later "King of Madagascar." [26] Benyowsky was killed in 1786.

Thus the three centuries following the "discovery" of Madagascar by Diogo Diaz seem to have been marked by greater or lesser attempts along the coasts and in the south to reduce the state of insecurity through new forms of government, beginning with confederation and ending, by means of conquest, with kingdoms. Some of the kingdoms were highly involved and complex structures. Others do not merit the designation "kingdom." Some of the attempts were extremely successful, others failed. Two features were common to all: The creation of new forms of government was the work of individuals, and the role of these individuals was apparently nontransferable beyond the immediate offspring. There was, however, one exception.

THE MERINA

In the very heart of Madagascar, the once-insignificant tribe of Antimerina was rapidly increasing. Blessed with a favorable climate and protected by forests and the high plateau on which they lived, the Merina soon came to challenge the rest of the Malagasy tribes for supremacy. Their noble clans, predominantly of Indo-Melanesian stock, slowly imposed themselves on the darker populations—the Vazimba, Antehiroka, and others. Beginning with one of the first queens, Rafohy, who ruled the valley of the Siasony River from Imerimanjaka in the first half of the sixteenth century, through the reigns of Andriamanelo at the end of the sixteenth century, and those of Ralambo and Andrianjaka as well as several lesser monarchs in the seventeenth century until about 1780, the noble clans (*Andriana*) extended their power throughout the central plateau. It was a slow expansion and consolidation, far less spectacular than the growth of Menabé and Boina. Moreover, the *Andriana* were by no means united. Succession to the throne was a hazardous undertaking, involving assassination and exile.

In 1787, a great Merina monarch, Andrianampoinimerina, nominally acceded to the throne. It took him ten years to unify the whole of the central plateau under his rule. By 1810, his army was in control of a large chunk of high-plateau regions from Tananarive to Fianarantsoa, spilling into the Tanala Ikongo and

Menabé kingdoms. "Nampoina," as some historians call him, did not stop merely with conquest. The social and economic organization of the Merina rested on stratification by classes. First, there were the nobles. They furnished the queens and the kings as well as the royal entourage, "the Court." Their combined power was usually greater than that of the previous monarchs. It was also recognized as such. For example, a Merina king who ruled from about 1675 to 1710 frequently addressed the *Andriana* by saying that it is "for us all to make decisions, and not merely myself." The *Andriana* were further subdivided into lesser and greater nobles, the first being *petits seigneurs* and the second the *Menakely*, or near and distant members of the royal house. Next came the *Hova-mainty*, or free men. As merchants, traders, and cultivators as well as artisans, the *Hova-mainty* were comparable to the middle class, with those enjoying the favor of the royal house forming the upper-middle class. Finally, there were the slaves, divided into four categories: the *Hova-vao*, or privileged slaves; the *Zaza-Hova*, or former free men unable to pay their debts and reduced to temporary slavery; the *Tsiarondahy*, or royal slaves; and the *Andevo*, or the slave caste from which there was almost no escape. As in the ancient Greek polis, the slaves were taken for granted, a part of life. The first three categories were rather well treated, often as members of the family. The lot of the *Andevo* was harsher.

By harnessing the *Andriana* and the *Hova-mainty*, Nampoina was able to establish an administrative system of lasting value. Before his death in 1810, the organization of the Merina state was as follows:

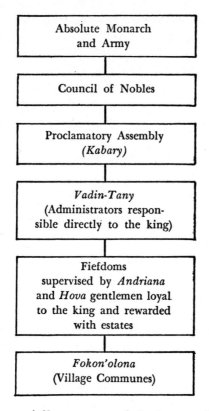

| Absolute Monarch and Army |
| Council of Nobles |
| Proclamatory Assembly *(Kabary)* |
| *Vadin-Tany* (Administrators responsible directly to the king) |
| Fiefdoms supervised by *Andriana* and *Hova* gentlemen loyal to the king and rewarded with estates |
| *Fokon'olona* (Village Communes) |

This was essentially a system of dual control, as can be seen from the following rearrangement:

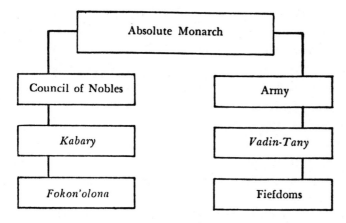

The monarchy had become a source of real power based on patronage and charism, which passed from Andrianampoinimerina to the throne itself. Moreover, to ensure a strong successor, he groomed his son Radama, the young general of the Merina army. Radama was kept away from the Court on military campaigns. He returned to Tananarive to succeed his father in 1810. On his deathbed, Nampoina left Radama I a legacy of far-reaching implications, expressed in the sentence *"Ny riaka no valamparihiko,"* which means, "The sea is the limit of my rice fields."

Both Radama I (1810–28) and Queen Ranavalona I (1828–61) sought to extend Merina supremacy throughout Madagascar, the sea being the limit. Excluding parts of Sakalava territory and the southern part of the island, they successfully carried out the mandate of Nampoina. No two rulers in the known history of Madagascar, particularly in the history of the Merina state, could have been more different, and yet each reflected major trends surviving to this day in Malagasy society.[27] For almost two decades, Radama I stressed the positive aspects of Western civilization. It is under his rule that missionary schools were opened. *Malgache* became a written language and several thousand Malagasy became literate. Radama I surrounded himself with European advisers. Some of his subjects were even sent abroad to study. His army was modernized. New crafts began to flourish. Trade and commerce experienced an unprecedented boom. He was not keen on Christianity, but was quick to borrow some of its aspects, which made it easier to break away from many of the *fady,* or restrictive customs, that made no sense in the "new era." French and English missionaries were given complete freedom of proselytization. In foreign policy, Radama I tended to favor the British. This was largely due to the work of Sir Robert Farquhar, the Governor of nearby Mauritius, and Hastie, his personal agent. The pro-British policy was assured by a treaty concluded in October, 1817, whereby Britain recognized Radama I as King of Madagascar. Unity and material progress, innovation and the readiness to avoid isolationism, and a belief in education made Radama I a precursor of many current Malagasy as well as African leaders.

Ranavalona I represents an altogether different tendency. Hostile to outside influences, she carried out reprisals against the missionaries, both Protestant and Catholic. She surrounded herself with courtiers rather than foreign advisers. Her rule marked the ascendancy of a mixed *Andriana-Hova* plutocracy—composed of military chiefs, gentlemen, and wealthy traders—and a return to orthodoxy, the *fady*, and fetishism. In isolationism, orthodoxy, and oligarchy, the Merina were beginning to resemble the Amharic kingdom of Ethiopia. Ranavalona's regressive reign was mitigated by the emergence of three interesting figures who sought to alter the course of the Merina state. One was Rainiharo. Of royal blood, he was in charge of a foreign policy marked by a considerable degree of realism. He sent delegations to both London and Paris, fearing that a possible Franco-British alliance might spell foreign conquest for Madagascar (a view which was confirmed as accurate several decades later). Rainiharo also had a French protégé who became a Malagasy citizen and who may be said to have brought the first modern industrial establishment to Madagascar. His name was Jean Laborde. In a factory of 1,000 apprentices at Mantasoa, this unique Frenchman seems to have manufactured almost everything from cannons (some of which are historical treasures of the Malagasy Republic) to pottery, from soap to rum. Even the Queen herself was impressed and gave Laborde a high rank at her Court.

Rainiharo died in 1852. A second innovator was Queen Ranavalona's own son, Rakoto, a young man whose idols were Radama I and Laborde. The first was his real father; the second, his mentor and father by adoption. Physically frail and highly idealistic, Rakoto became Radama II in 1861, following the death of his mother. Radama II surprised everyone. Instead of executing those who conspired against him, he gave them liberty. He abolished the death penalty. He returned prisoners from other tribes to their homes. He proclaimed total freedom of worship. He equated Christianity with civilization itself. Highly pro-French, Radama II signed a treaty of "perpetual friendship" with France in 1862, and was in turn recognized as King of Madagascar. Frenchmen were allowed to buy Merina lands and settle in Madagascar. And he accepted a feature of the *capitulations,* or extraterritorial-privilege system, whereby French citizens could be subjected to trial only by their own diplomatic representatives. It was not long before the vested interests of the plutocracy intervened, and Radama II was assassinated in 1863.

It was a third figure, Rainilaiarivony, a confidant of Ranavalona I and husband of Queen Rasoherina (1863–68) as well as of Queen Ranavalona II (1868–83), who brought about the most significant reforms since Nampoina and Radama I. As Prime Minister, Rainilaiarivony modernized the administration. He broke the power of the nobles, created a bureaucratic apparatus under a group of ministries, and bypassed the fiefs by setting up a direct system of royal functionaries, or *Sakaizambohitra*.* In foreign policy, Rainilaiarivony sought a balance of power, playing off the British against the French, and vice versa. A shrewd analyst of power factors, he was able to check his anti-French sentiment in spite of Protestant pressures † and the work of his British army instructors—Lovett, Onbeline, Parett (who served as a mediator at the Sakalava stronghold of Majunga), and Willoughby (who was made commander in chief of the Merina army).[28] The ministries he created were: Interior (five departments); Foreign Affairs; War (five districts); Justice (eight departments); Commerce, Industry, and Public Works (five directorates); Finance (four departments); Legislation (two departments); and Public Education (six sectors).

Some have assumed that the British had a hand in the establishment of these European-type ministries, particularly since, at that time, many French diplomats in European capitals were agitating against the "dictatorial state of affairs" in Madagascar, preparing the ground for an eventual French invasion of the island. Moreover, French claims were based on "coastal protectorates" in Madagascar and on the factual consideration that, beyond the high-plateau regions, Merina rule over the island was more theoretical than real. Merina territory covered thousands of square miles, and they had

* *Sakaizambohitra* literally means "friends of the village." They were charged with the task of hearing complaints and keeping registers, called *Bokimpanjakana*. Like the Ottoman *harshorids* (inspectors responsible directly to the Sultan), the *Sakaizambohitra* were an instrument of direct administration, assigned to break the power of feudal fiefs unwilling to submit to central authority.

† The English Protestants gained strong favor with Ranavalona II, who, by a royal decree of February 21, 1869, proclaimed the Protestant Church as the official church of the Merina state.

to contend with a whole galaxy of more or less un-friendly vassal tribes. Yet the evidence does not support the assumption that the ministries were a foreign creation. They were, without question, based on Eu-ropean models, but in terms of actual function they operated clearly within the customs, mores, and struc-ture of Malagasy society. After years in power, Rainilaiarivony realized that administrative moderniza-tion was the only way to preserve Merina supremacy, already severely taxed by rebellions and corruption.

In his late years, with all of his prowess, this astute Merina statesman failed to see the handwriting on the wall. He well understood the dangers from within the island, but not those from without. By the mid-1880's, under pretext of a dispute with Queen Ranavalona III (1883–97), the French sent their first punitive expedition to Madagascar. The Queen was forced to sign a treaty whereby the French recognized the sovereignty of the Merina state in exchange for control of its foreign affairs, an indemnity payment of 10 million francs, and rights over the port of Diego-Suarez. What ensued was a struggle on two levels. Locally, the Merina refused to adhere to the treaty provisions and waged a small-scale war against the French as well as against rebelling tribes. Internationally, the fate of Madagascar was sealed. "A colonial agreement was made. The French recognized the British protectorate in Zanzibar and the supremacy which the activity of the Royal Niger Com-pany had secured for Great Britain in the Haussa states. [In return] Salisbury recognized the French protectorate in Madagascar, which had been virtually established by the treaty of December, 1885, and accepted the hinter-land of Algeria as coming within the French sphere of influence." [29] The French, under General Duchesne, occupied Tananarive in September, 1895. Exiled to Algeria, Rainilaiarivony died in 1896. His last wife, Queen Ranavalona III, also died in exile in Algeria twenty-one years later.

History cannot tell us what might have happened had the French not occupied the island of Madagascar. It cannot be denied that in the nineteenth century the Merina were on the way toward establishing a Malagasy state. Another young Radama I, or a Rainilaiarivony, or a combination of both, might have succeeded. Nor, despite frequent authoritarian rulers, can it be said that there were no democratic institutions. One of them, the *Fokon'olona*, or village community cooperative, has been revived during the last decade, after a long period of inactivity. In certain aspects the *Fokon'olona* can be compared to an early stage of *Zadruga,* or house community, among the Balkan Slavs. Under the guidance of a headman (*mpiatidy*), every member of the village cooperative takes part in its management, who, in turn, is responsible to the council of village elders—men and women most advanced in years and called *Raya'mandreny* (fathers and mothers). A statute (*Fanekempokon'olona*) is drawn up either on paper or, more often, orally (committed to memory and recited by a member). Once accepted by the *Raya'mandreny,* an agreement by statute becomes a law binding all members of the village cooperative. Historically, *Fokon'olona* has been a miniature producing-consuming organization as well as a commune, with its own government and laws. The *Kabary* was another partly democratic institution. The *Kabary* (literally, "discourse") was actually no more democratic than a given ruler allowed it to be. On the one level, an ordinary subject could submit grievances to the king without fear of punishment at a *Kabary*. On another, and more prevalent, level, the *Kabary* served as a gathering place or a communications center where important proclamations were made and disseminated among large crowds. An account by Reverend Cousins in 1877 illustrates the wider meaning of *Kabary*:

> The greatest political event of the year has been the emancipation of the Mozambique slaves. As far back as October, 1874, a proclamation was issued by the Malagasy Government freeing all Mozambiques imported into Madagascar since the completion of the treaty with Great Britain in 1865. . . . This proclamation failed, however, to effect any satisfactory results, and the Queen, guided by the counsel of Rainilaiarivony, Prime Minister and Commander in Chief, determined to take a bold progressive step and liberate all the Mozambiques in the island, whether imported or born here. This was accomplished on June 20 of this year. A grand *Kabary* was held in the capital, and on the same day similar gatherings were held on a smaller scale at all the ports and garrison-towns throughout the Queen's dominions. The Royal Proclamation was read in the capital by Rainilaiarivony.[30]

Malagasy society, perhaps like any other, was and is neither wholly democratic nor wholly authoritarian. It harbors both tendencies; the only question is which tendency will prevail in the end. The kingdoms of Menabé and Boina, Betsimisaraka or Isandra—not to mention lesser ones—never transcended purely regional arrangements. The great Imerina Kingdom never became a full Malagasy state. It remained for the colonial period to bring about the last stage of political evolution.

II

ADMINISTRATION
AND REVOLT: 1897-1947

The Lone Administrator

During the colonial expansion between the 1880's and the turn of the century, several individuals of high caliber were sent to European possessions in Africa and elsewhere. One such individual was General Joseph S. Gallieni, who came to Madagascar in 1896 as its first governor general. (It is not without political irony that, in France, Gallieni is chiefly remembered as the ingenious general who, in World War I, rushed troops to the frontlines in taxicabs.) Corsican by birth, French to the core, Malagasy by virtue of his genuine concern for the people, and, above all, republican by deep conviction, Gallieni brought with him rich experience and a profound sense of humanity. While still a young captain in the French army, he had been captured by Sultan Ahmadu, the Sardauna of Sokoto. After ten months of imprisonment, Gallieni not only won his freedom, but induced the Sultan to sign a friendship treaty with France. For several years thereafter, Gallieni explored the Niger River and held the post of military commander of the French Sudan. Gallieni respected scholarship and often sought academic advice on matters of importance. Among his early acts as governor was an administrative order to all personnel to gather facts about every aspect of the Malagasy, from their history to their social structure.

Upon his arrival in Madagascar, Gallieni was faced with a host of immediate problems, some of which may be singled out as being of major importance. One of the precepts Gallieni shared with virtually every Frenchman concerned with the island of Madagascar was the conviction that France was liberating most Malagasy from the Merina yoke. Hence, the first problem was to eliminate Merina feudalism and hegemony. The military victory had merely terminated armed resistance; it had not removed the administrative hold of the *Andriana* and *Hova-mainty* over a large number of non-Merina. The second major task was to implement the decree of June, 1896, which abolished slavery in Madagascar, at least theoretically. This was a delicate and complex problem. In spite of the proclamations of Queen Ranavalona II on the emancipation of slaves, close to 30 per cent of the population were, in fact, little better than slaves. The economic institution of slavery was not exclusively a Merina practice. Moreover, among the Meina, some of the slaves—the *Hova-vao* and *Tsiarondahy*—were trusted domestic servants who would not leave the household, even if officially freed. The great weakness of the abolition proclamation was not a lack of enforcement facilities, but the paying of only lip service to missionary ideals. The few thousand slaves who were freed here and there either drifted slowly back into slavery or remained free because no "employment" could be found for them.

The third problem facing Gallieni was connected with a policy principle of the Colonial Ministry in Paris: i.e., that colonial administrations be self-sustaining.[1] In practical terms this meant that the Malagasy would have to be taxed if the administration was to receive revenues. The problem of revenue was further magnified by France's mercantilistic policy. More than a century had passed since the physiocrats had advocated *"Laissez faire et laissez passer, le monde va de lui-même."* But Paris was still impressed by the idea of a favorable balance of trade.* A high ad-valorem tax on all foreign goods, imposed by France, almost killed foreign trade for Madagascar. In a letter to Joseph Chailley,[2] Secretary-General of the Union Coloniale, Gallieni demanded stiffer economic measures against both American merchants and French commercial *sociétés*, some of which had been in Madagascar since the time of Radama I. (This should be understood not only in terms of revenue, but also in terms of the fact that Gallieni wanted to prevent the premature colonization of Madagascar.) [3] In the same letter, he went on to add that he would agree to permit foreign private enterprises to establish themselves in Madagascar, but only if there was willingness on their part to build roads and communications and to pay adequate wages to locally recruited labor. He concluded that several foreign companies had agreed to these terms provided Paris would guarantee that their properties would be protected, but that "unfortunately, the [Colonial] Department seems hardly disposed to agree with my recommendations." [4] The obvious ambivalence of Gallieni in economic mat-

---

* The favorable balance-of-trade outlook was discarded only in the 1948–50 period. Prior to 1948, even conservative students of Malagasy affairs contended that such an outlook could no longer be maintained. As Pierre Launois wrote in 1947: "The old colonial treaty of Colbert must no longer be permitted to regulate the relations between metropolitan France and her overseas territories." (*Op. cit.*, p. 245.)

ters (on the one hand, he wanted to impose higher taxes on foreign enterprise, while on the other, he wanted to attract private capital to Madagascar) led to charges of economic opportunism. That these were unfounded becomes apparent upon closer examination of the man, his writings, and his relationships. If anything, this was a man whose conscience was torn between policies that would primarily benefit metropolitan France and those that would keep Malagasy interests uppermost. This dual loyalty of Gallieni has been traced to his desire to unify the island both politically and economically, a desire that grew out of his emulation of Radama I. No subsequent governor of Madagascar can be said to have been preoccupied with the problem of dual loyalty. At any rate, the refusal of Paris to offer the requested guarantees led to an appreciable lessening of commercial interest in the island—an interest that was hard to stimulate in the first place because of the distance between Madagascar and Europe.

Gallieni's fourth task was to pacify the still-rebellious parts of Madagascar, particularly the south.[5] The last major problem was that of ending the quarrels between Catholic and Protestant missionaries—quarrels not only of a religious nature but having political overtones as well. The Protestants had always represented the prestige of Great Britain; the Catholics, that of France. The political aspect of religious competition was therefore a "lag" traceable to the Anglo-French rivalry that had ended with the fall of Tananarive in 1895. Fortunately, the conflict had never reached the proportions existing in Uganda at that time. In dealing with all these problems, it should be mentioned that Gallieni did not have an entirely free hand to do what he wanted. In October, 1896, he wrote to Alfred Grandidier:

> In my opinion, I should not be burdened with formalities at the present time, formalities that tend to stifle everything. If freedom of action is not allowed me I would rather pass my present responsibilities to someone else. I have no idea how long they'll let me stay here, but it is my belief that if left alone, I should be able to report a fairly good situation here in a year or two.[6]

Gallieni solved the first problem initially through an effective use of military organization. Dividing the island into military districts (*cercles*), he forced the Merina functionaries and fiefs to work under his officers and noncommissioned personnel. In addition, Gallieni sought the help of local chiefs by proclaiming the principle of equality of all tribes in January, 1897. During Resident-General Laroche's term (1895–96), an all-French administrative advisory council combining military, paramilitary, and civilian personnel, had been established. Gallieni also made full use of this by simply placing some Malagasy elders on the council. Thus, Gallieni attained two goals. He controlled the island and won the esteem and cooperation of many chiefs through his principle of tribal equality (which French scholars have called the *politique des races, races* in this context meaning "tribes," not "races"). Gallieni thought that the Merina were thus removed from power while continuing to perform useful functions; in this he was to be proved wrong.

It took some ingenuity to carry out the abolition decree, but Gallieni was equal to the task. Four days after he took over from Laroche, Gallieni ordered that

"All unemployed males between the ages of sixteen and sixty must give fifty days of labor each year upon public works or convoys." [7] Three months later, he ordered all concerned to show evidence of employment. Failure to produce such evidence led to imprisonment or paid work on public roads. Since slavery was illegal, and since slaves could not provide evidence of genuine employment (the certificates being issued by French authorities), they were "arrested" and put to work on roads. After fifty days of paid labor they were released but could opt to remain as "volunteers" in public-works gangs. There is no evidence to suggest that Gallieni used pressure to force ex-slaves to become "volunteers," but whatever the case may have been, the men were unquestionably better off and were able to find means of livelihood, without which most of them would almost certainly have gone back into some "legal" form of slavery. At the same time, Gallieni was improving and building roads, without which neither the control nor the economic development of Madagascar could have been effected.

The problem of taxation was attacked next by Gallieni through the use of *Fokon'olona* among the Betsileo and Merina and village councils elsewhere.[8] The utilization of Malagasy institutions by Gallieni has been regarded as political opportunism. It was contended that, given the small army of 1,500 French regulars and 5,000 Senegalese and Malagasy auxiliaries under his command, he was unable to control 228,000 square miles of territory, and that instead of asking for more men he "manipulated native institutions." These charges originated among some powerful military interests as well as among proponents of "assimilation," who included some missionaries as well. In fact, Gallieni's use of Malagasy institutions reflected a concept far more significant than either assimilation or indirect rule, based as it was on Herbert Spencer's concept of "natural development" or decentralized administration that guides social change but does not "create" it. Thus the revenues Gallieni collected through taxes applied beyond the narrow confines of administrative self-support.

The "pacification" of Madagascar took about seven years, the last organized resistance in the south being brought to an end in 1905. What the Merina had sought to accomplish throughout the nineteenth century thus took place in less than a decade. But here Gallieni's otherwise unblemished record received its only black mark. In spite of his orders prohibiting the destruction of villages and indiscriminate reprisals under penalty of general court-martial, there were instances of needless bloodshed that went unpunished. In the old Menabé, for example, the stronghold of a minor ruler was destroyed, and, though about to surrender, he was put to death. Gallieni never punished the commander of that expedition. On the whole, however, there were few major reprisals. Most tribes submitted to control, and their chiefs were returned to power as members of the new administration. Another regrettable act was to permit the War Council to condemn to death and execute the uncle of Queen Ranavalona and one of her ministers—the ostensible reason being that they were "leaders of a rebellion against France." Actually, the military leaders of this rebellion were released and went free. The uncle of Ranavalona and the minister were executed to frighten the restless Merina ruling circles into submission. The uncle was an *Andriana;* the minister a *Hova* of high rank. Yet the successful end did not justify the harsh means. More patient and less severe ways could have achieved much the same result. The two executions were hardly characteristic of Gallieni's methods. While it is true that the War Council's decision was made only two weeks after Gallieni came to Madagascar, the question of why he did not overrule that body remains unexplained.

Shortly before Gallieni landed in Madagascar, Resident-General Laroche (himself a French Protestant) had passed an executive order guaranteeing complete religious freedom to both the Catholic and Protestant churches. Gallieni did not revise or amend the order, but his concern with the reduction of English influences in Malagasy education led him to decree that all school children were to be taught in French. This irked the Protestants. To lessen friction, Gallieni invited a group of French Protestants to Madagascar. This measure was resented both by the French Catholics and the English Protestants. In placing the interests of state above all others, Gallieni was subjected to considerable criticism, and pressure was brought on the clergy in Paris to have him removed from office. In this they did not succeed, largely because of anticlericalism in France itself. Gallieni, however, failed to reconcile and mollify the missionary interests in Madagascar.

On the strength of three achievements alone, Gallieni may be said to have laid the foundations of the future Malagasy state. The military pacification reduced the state of insecurity that had sapped local energies for hundreds of years throughout the island. Administratively, he came close to unifying Madagascar for the first time in history without creating bitter enemies. Although Gallieni was born on a different island, it was he who, in the final analysis, carried out the political mandate of King Andrianampoinimerina. Where others had merely advocated and proclaimed the abolition of slavery, Gallieni found a way to accomplish it. Its permanent abolition did not alter the agricultural structure of Malagasy society, but it did pave the way toward an eventual republic, for economically, both the Merina monarchy and Merina oligarchy had depended heavily on slavery. Also of far-reaching implications was Gallieni's principle of tribal equality (*politique des races*), the aim of which, according to a speech he delivered shortly before his departure from Madagascar, was:

> To reverse and dilute the barriers that separate the various tribal populations of the island, to foster the fusion of tribes in an association of interests, to effect in sum an exchange of produce and of ideas that will, in the end, permit the realization of a political and administrative unity.[9]

Certainly the least that can be said on Gallieni's behalf is that he occupies a unique place in the history of Franco-Malagasy relations. Even the most vehement critics of French policy in Madagascar admit that much. In many books written by Frenchmen of differing political convictions between the two world wars, pleas were to be found for a return to Gallieni's policies. It took a major revolt to revive them.

4

The Machine Takes Over

The two governors that followed Gallieni, Victor Augagneur (1905–10) and Albert Picquié (1910–14), each, in his own way, set out to change the pattern of administration. Augagneur, who was considerably to the "left" in French politics and distrusted the military, abolished the mixed military-civilian system of decentralized administration.[1] His new structure proved far more expensive, and in order to cut the costs, he reduced educational "overhead." At the expense of the rest of the island, Augagneur limited his interests, both economical and administrative, to the central-plateau regions. Apart from some work on railroad expansion and an initial attempt to improve irrigation and drainage around Lake Alaotra (both of which measures benefited the *colons* and one or two corporations) Augagneur's term in office brought neither economic nor social improvements to the Malagasy. Ignorant of the history of Madagascar and hence of its basic problems, Augagneur made it possible for the Merina slowly to return to power—this time under the aegis of the French administration. Picquié had no axes to grind. Long accustomed to bureaucratic life as an official of the Colonial Ministry, his main worry was to please Paris by not bringing up any problems, or at least as few as possible. He balanced the budget, lorded it over the Merina functionaries, and upon his departure in 1914, left only one major memento of his tenure: the railroad station in Tananarive. What Augagneur had begun, Picquié consolidated.

The upheavals of World War I did not bypass Madagascar. The Allied war machine required soldiers, laborers, and food supplies. Madagascar was drained steadily by the indiscriminate exportation of consumer goods. Scarcities led to black markets, profiteering, and exploitation. According to official figures, 45,863 Malagasy "volunteers" were recruited (41,355 were combat troops and 4,508 labor support), and most of them were sent overseas. Many of the pastoral Malagasy were forced to sell livestock at heavily reduced prices to "help the war effort." Graphite, of which Madagascar was and still is one of the largest producers in the world, was shipped out by the thousands of tons without any benefit accruing to local economies, regional or otherwise. The wartime unconcern for the Malagasy can be further adduced from the rapid turnover of governors: Garbit (1914–17), Merlin (1917–18), Scharmech (1918–19), and Guyon (1919–20).

The "war effort" led to considerable bitterness among the Malagasy and to the first stirrings of nationalism, which, to some extent, transcended tribal and regional lines. Toward the end of Augagneur's governorship, a small group of mission-educated Merina students led by Reverend Ravelojaona founded an equivalent of the YMCA in Tananarive. Informed of group discussions that might possibly oppose the interests of the administration, Augagneur abolished the YMCA as a part of his "savings" campaign. Within two years (about 1912–13), the students formed a secret society for the "preservation of the cultural heritage," which, somewhat later, was given the name Vy Vato ("stone and iron"—symbols of purity and discipline). With the war intruding into the life of the island, the students divided into sections, or *Sakelika,* and the society came to be known as VVS (Vy Vato Sakelika). It had several hundred members, including some non-Merina. Besides Reverend Ravelojaona, the VVS's reputed leaders were two young priests, Manifatra and Rafiringa, and a student of medicine at Tananarive's Medical College, Joseph Ravoahangy. Meeting in Tananarive in the early part of December, 1915, the VVS plotted to "throw the French out of Madagascar" —an ambitious, although unrealistic, plan. The news of the meeting leaked out, and on December 24, 1915, Garbit's police began a wave of arrests; a few days later, some 500 Malagasy students were in jail. Following a sensational trial in February, 1916, and without any real proof of alleged "poisoning plots" (whereby all the French were to be poisoned at the same time), eight students were condemned to life imprisonment at forced labor, and another twenty-six received sentences ranging from twenty to five years of forced labor. A few days later, Garbit ordered another 170 students sent to the penal camp of Nosy-Lava on the west coast. Some of the students were under sixteen years of age. Ravoahangy and another medical student, Raseta, were in their late teens.

With the end of the war, conditions began to improve

somewhat. Garbit became governor for the second time. During his second term (1920–24), Garbit instituted an administrative reform that, luckily, was reversed by his successor. Briefly, it was a reorganization that could not fail to perpetuate tribal divisions. Twenty-three provinces, based on tribal regions, were created under the direction of a Consultative Committee for Native Affairs consisting of five Frenchmen and six Malagasy— all six *Hova* favoring the administration. In addition, Garbit called a Congress for Economic Affairs, which included one Malagasy from each of the twenty-two provinces. The Congress idea originated with the Tananarive Chamber of Commerce in an effort to increase Malagasy-*colon* cooperation. Postwar demand had led to a minor boom in agriculture, and Malagasy farmers and sharecroppers were finding that working one's own land was more profitable than working land that belonged to someone else. The prices for agricultural produce increased much faster than the wages that could be earned. Possibly the best description on this aspect of the period (1923–26) has been given by H. I. Priestley.

> During the prosperity of 1924–25, agricultural exports reached such high prices that the natives deserted the French to work for themselves, because crops raised in a few weeks paid better than work for wages would have done in a year. Wages only doubled, but prices quintupled, and yet employers complained that profits would disappear if the wage scale were raised. The only remedy lay in stimulating natives to work. . . .
>
> Many colonists have come to be solicitous for the welfare of their laborers, if not for humane reasons at least from self-interest. It seems that the best laborers have

sought government employ, and Olivier [Governor from
1924–29] used them as examples by raising their wages
to encourage emulation. His labor legislation, based on
an exhaustive investigation of regional needs, convinced
him that the problem was not of mere labor legislation,
but complete transformation of the economic structure,
which could be effected only after long time. The essential feature of the new law was the assumption that
normal labor should be voluntary, but under control of
labor offices; but all work of three months' duration must
be under contract approved by the government. Ficti-
tious contracts [made to avoid forced labor] were made
punishable by fine and imprisonment. Inspection of labor
was taken from the administrators of districts, who had
often been both parties and judges of disputes, and given
to special officers. The procedure of labor arbitration
boards was speeded up, and judgments favoring natives
given easier execution. The code also made rules for re-
patriation, wages, medical care, lodging, clothing, and
elimination of abuses, at the same time protecting em-
ployers against labor supply that is unstable and unre-
liable. The outstanding feature is the function of the
regional labor offices to assist and control recruiting for
public and private work. This is the first time the administration has departed from the theoretical principle
of neutrality and of free labor; but without pressure nine
tenths of the European developments would fail for lack
of workers, while crops would be wasted unless labor
could be legally recruited at the critical moments. . . . In
1926, the compulsion of labor was placed in the care of
the Service de la Main-d'Oeuvre pour les Travaux d'In-
térêt Général (SMOTIG).[2]

Many people, including Frenchmen, criticized the
whole idea that led to the SMOTIG. According to J.
Goudal:

No such thing as forced labor existed in any colonial code of legislation, but there was the "moral obligation" to work in Portuguese colonies, "administrative aid" in Belgian colonies, "respect for the customary rights of the chiefs" in British colonies, *prestations,* "authorization of recruiting," and the "second class of military contingents" in French colonies.[3]

Governor Marcel Olivier (1924–29) defended the SMOTIG after his term expired in Madagascar before an International Labor Conference in Geneva against the charge that it claimed "a million victims in 1928" by offering evidence that, in 1928, there were actually only 7,957 laborers under it, with only 68 deaths, and that while this kind of labor was badly needed for the improvement of communications, the wages were comparatively high and the men received adequate care.[4] The above-mentioned figure was confirmed later in a study by the (British) Royal Institute of International Affairs, with the following statement:

[The] French system . . . includes a scheme first devised by M. Olivier when Governor of Madagascar, for the employment of those men liable to military service but not enrolled in the Army, who may form mobile labor battalions, living under military conditions. This "second contingent" may be employed in public works, and in some private enterprise, the period of service being two years. In Madagascar the number of men so enrolled in 1929 was 10,000; in 1930, arrangements were made to enroll voluntary labor on similar lines.[5]

The volunteer arrangements were instituted by Governor Léon Cayla (1930–39), and he used the SMOTIG with the approval of the International Labour Office. It should be added that famine in the south dislodged thousands, and that one way to find employment was to volunteer for the SMOTIG. The SMOTIG was abolished in 1936, but here again the early 1930's were the years of economic slump, and the private sector of the economy had no trouble finding workers.

Of all the governors who followed Gallieni, Marcel Olivier is the only one who, to some extent, reverted to the policies of the 1896–1905 period. Olivier abolished the tribal division implemented by Garbit. Instead of twenty-three, there were now six provinces, subdivided into forty-four districts. The real change, or rather return to the 1896–1905 period, was that several smaller tribes were put into a single province, while the larger ones were "split" between the provinces, a division that fostered internal migration and weakened the tribal structure. The Garbit division, if allowed to remain, would have led to the kind of system adopted by Belgium in the Congo—in other words, to the preservation of tribal regionalism beneath the structure of a modern administrative apparatus. Another promising, but less effective, contribution by Olivier was the creation of the Economic and Financial Delegations (EFD) by a decree of May 7, 1924. Evolving out of the former Consultative Committee for Native Affairs, the EFD had two sections; the first consisted of twelve French citizens elected by chambers of commerce in principal towns, with another twelve elected by six constituencies. The indigenous section also had twenty-four members, elected by the notables of each district council. While the EFD acted only in an advisory capacity, it was consulted initially on matters of budgets and public loans and works. The EFD was another aspect of the concept of effective government through decentralization. Six months after the establishment of the EFD, on December 25, 1924, a law was passed authorizing the governor-general to delegate his powers (including budgetary powers) to provincial heads.[6]

There are, however, significant differences between Gallieni and Olivier. The European element in Madagascar was not well organized or particularly extensive in Gallieni's time. Olivier, on the other hand, had to contend with powerful pressure groups reaching all the way to Paris. Moreover, Olivier faced no problem of "dual loyalty." The founding of the Crédit Agricole and the Banque de Madagascar, the regulations regarding land tenure (decree of September 28, 1926), as well as the creation of *contremaîtres de culture* for both public and private employment in new agrarian schools like those at Ivoloina, Tamatave, and Anstirabé—all of these were measures aimed at helping the colonial economy first and foremost. Gallieni had used the forced fifty days of labor primarily to demolish a feudal system economically based on slavery. The building of roads was a by-product. Olivier's SMOTIG was used to protect the *colons* and *sociétés* from the hazards of a free labor market based on demand. To Gallieni, decentralization meant a two-way flow between central and local authorities in almost every aspect. Olivier worked from the top down on important matters, allowing the two-way flow only where his span of control was weak.

The administration of Léon Cayla, which followed that of Olivier, was marked not so much by any significant or far-reaching reforms as by two extremely important trends: neglect of public education and an increas-

ingly effective centralization. If the administration during the 1930's were to be judged by the sheer number of
proposals for improvements, decrees, and flattering remarks about Cayla in contemporary writings, it could
be said that this decade constituted the most progressive
period in the colonial history of Madagascar prior to
World War II. The two trends, however, are overshadowed by a morass of legalism, formality, and
bureaucratic ritual.

In 1931, there were 959 public schools in Madagascar,
with a total enrollment of 110,928.* Ninety-four per
cent of these schools and 98 per cent of the student body
were in the realm of primary education. Between 1931
and 1939, only ninety new rural primary schools were
established, together with fourteen workshops and one
commercial-studies section for all of Madagascar. Thus
in 1940, only 130,082 students were enrolled in public
schools—an increase of less than 20,000 in a decade. At
the beginning of Cayla's administration in 1930, public
education in Madagascar was beset by two problems.
One was the problem of which language was to be
used in public schools, and the other was the very
uneven distribution of educational facilities throughout
the island. In so far as distribution was concerned, the
Merina, the Betsileo, and the Sihanaka enjoyed a great
advantage. The language of instruction in primary
public schools was Malagasy, with French taught as a
separate subject. The converse was true in the secondary
public schools and, in some cases, also in the last year
of primary school. The cause of this irrational compromise was the struggle between those who believed

---

* These figures do not include 244 Catholic and 237 Protestant
schools, with a total enrollment of 65,596.

that excessive use of French would carry with it the danger of too many "subversive ideas" and those who wanted to Frenchify the Malagasy children. The result of this compromise was that all too often the "educated" could not speak, read, or write either language well. Referring to this, a Malagasy educator remarked:

> Is this what is wanted in Madagascar? Slowly but surely . . . the effects are beginning to be felt. . . . Today only the old-timers know the language [Malagasy] well, and the more one descends down the scale of generations, the less one is apt to encounter a Malagasy capable of speaking his mother tongue correctly. As for the writing, it is better not to discuss the subject at all. . . . But, if the young people no longer speak Malagasy, do they at least speak French? It is here, alas, that the catastrophe can be determined in full. If you could only see those copies of the *baccalaureat!* Ideas? Yes, they have them—often more than their instructors; but what is one to call the gibberish in which they are expressed. . . .[7]

Cayla was not against "assimilation," but rather for its limitation to the select few who possessed French citizenship or to children of parents enjoying special status (*statut personnel*), which meant anyone so designated by the administration for a variety of reasons. The problem of language remained acute, and at least one third of the 105 new schools added to the educational establishment in the 1930's were built in the provinces of Tananarive and Fianarantsoa. The educational gap between the high plateau and the rest of Madagascar was thus widened.

A dual judicial organization was brought into legal being by a decree of July 17, 1926. Subject to the courts operating under the laws of metropolitan France were legal matters pertaining to "French citizens and non-French citizens who can prove foreign nationality." [8] "Assimilated" Malagasy, of whom there were only few, were considered foreigners living in Madagascar and thus came under the competence of the above courts. The rest of the Malagasy were subject to the *Code de l'Indigénat*, which allowed administrators to impose penalties for minor but fairly wide varieties of "offenses" without judicial review.[9] Offenses regarded as more serious were subject to judicial review in tribunals presided over by one European and two Malagasy and adhering to a mixture of Merina legislation and European imports, ranging from 305 articles of the Code of 1881 to the principle of *stare decisis*. The European and Malagasy magistrates often had no legal training.

The Olivier Administration had encouraged judicial review for minor offenses to prevent personal vendettas and arbitrary punishment. Some abuses did exist, but both the application of the law and its enforcement were rather lax. It was the Cayla Administration that altered the legal picture both in substance and in form. Instead of badly needed schools, ninety lower courts and thirty-nine higher courts were established throughout Madagascar by a decree of May 23, 1932. Administrative punishment of minor offenses became frequent. The ostensible reason for these measures was "a backlog of cases with which the previous legal establishment could not cope." The actual reason was to force the Malagasy to obey administrative measures affecting taxation, statutory labor, health, trade, and commerce. In the final analysis, the legal reforms are but one way to depict the trend of centralization.

The 1920's were highly significant for Madagascar from another point of view. Of some 34,000 Malagasy sent to the war theaters in Salonika and France, close to 3,000 did not return. They had died in a war that did not concern them, for a cause that was not theirs, and for a foreign country that ruled their own land. The 30,000 who did return were in many respects changed men. The economic "boom" of the 1920's absorbed most of them, but to many a member of the Nineteenth Battalion of the Malagasy Infantry, the colonial situation no longer made any sense. One of them, a former student who had narrowly missed being a member of the VVS by being drafted, decided to do something about it. His name was Jean Ralaimongo. While still in France, Ralaimongo helped organize the French League, which demanded that all Malagasy be granted French citizenship because of the contributions made by Madagascar to the war in Europe. The League's President was Anatole France, and its membership embraced an assortment of political orientations. Ralaimongo became its Adjunct Secretary and chief guiding spirit. His association with the League allowed him to meet personally with radicals, socialists, and communists. For example, while attending a congress of Action Coloniale in Tours, he shared a hotel room with a young Vietnamese named Ho Chi Minh.

From his European experience, Ralaimongo emerged as a Freemason and, what is more important, in the words of the poet Paul Niger, "Far from his country, far from his race—he found his country, he found his race." From the moment he returned to Madagascar in January, 1922, Ralaimongo became a thorn in the administration's flesh, a favorite target of the *petits colons* and ultraconservatives in Tananarive. In June, 1925, he was tried for having prevented a settler named Alidon from taking possession of some 3,000 acres of fertile land worked by Malagasy farmers in the district of Antalaha. Sent to prison for four months, Ralaimongo appealed the sentence and won his freedom in a retrial. Alidon refused to press charges, and the court of appeal had no choice but to dismiss the case. Alidon's act was apolitical. Of French peasant stock, he did not like the fact that the administration had given him a concession that was already being tilled by Malagasy farmers.* Ralaimongo's activities in the rural district of Antalaha (where he was forced to live by a decree of November 15, 1924, which allowed the administration to limit the residence of any Malagasy to a particular district) won him a certain amount of popularity. His legal fight and the trials, widely reported in the colonially oriented press, increased his popularity.

In 1927, together with Joseph Ravoahangy, the alleged VVS leader who had been released from forced labor in the Comoro Islands in 1922, he began to publish the newspaper *l'Opinion de Diego-Suarez*, which became the rallying point and the voice of a growing nationalist movement. Its demands were modest: "extension of French citizenship to all Malagasy on the basis of the Annexation Law of August 6, 1896," and the revision of the status of Madagascar "so that it can become a Department of France, such as Alsace-Lor-

---

* The problem stemmed from land-tenure laws that made unregistered lands the property of the state. The laws, of course, ignored both slash-and-burn farming—much as did the British in Kenya in the Kikuyu areas, a fact that may in part explain the Mau-Mau movement —and the possibility that even without *tavy*, there must have been thousands of Malagasy who, unaware of "legal" registration requirements, considered lands tilled by themselves as *their* lands.

raine, for example." [10] During the same year, a Russian-born lawyer from Diego-Suarez named Paul Dussac joined the staff of *l'Opinion.* Dussac had come to Madagascar in 1922 as a settler but, unable to make a living, he had become *"agent d'affaires,"* a euphemism for a lawyer who had not passed the bar. Later, Dussac moved to Tananarive and together with two Malagasy —Jules Ranaivo and Emmanuel Razafindrakoto— founded *l'Aurore Malgache.* Shortly after the founding of *l'Aurore,* two more Europeans joined the growing movement: Édouard Planque and François Vittori. Both happened to have been Communists.

Neither Garbit (who during his first gubernatorial term had suppressed the VVS) nor Olivier cared much for the nationalist movement or for the French League. Both harassed its individual members but made no attempt to suppress the movement itself. Early in 1929, Olivier left the island and Berthier took over as interim governor until the arrival of Léon Cayla. On May 19, 1929, demonstrations broke out in Tananarive. About 4,000 Malagasy marched through the streets loudly demanding French citizenship. The following day, about thirty demonstrators were arrested. All but Planque and Vittori were released. Soon after his arrival in January, 1930, however, Cayla crushed the movement without hesitation. Using the *Code Indigènat* and additional administrative decrees, Cayla dispersed scores of activists throughout the island. Others were arrested and detained indefinitely. *L'Opinion* was closed down, and Ralaimongo was confined to Port Bergé. Ravoahangy was sent to Maintirano on the west coast. Dussac was transferred from the Tananarive to the Majunga prison.

The late 1920's were the time of Communist agitation and of the "Red scare" in Europe. Hence, Ralaimongo's association with some Communists in France, Dussac's Russian birth, and the Communist Party affiliation of Planque and Vittori were sufficient to lead some people to assume that the movement itself was Red. The administration did not fully accept this view, but it would not tolerate even a comparatively mild and embryonic "nationalist movement," the only major demand of which was French citizenship for all Malagasy. The suppression proved to be one of the costliest errors that could possibly have been made. At the time, however, few understood the wider implications of Cayla's repressive policies. Some did not even understand them two decades later. Thus a French scholar, writing in 1952, was able to assert:

> Since 1928, an agitation of nationalist tendency made its mark, an agitation that as early as May 19, 1929, resulted in a public demonstration. By means of several stern measures, the new Chief [Cayla] put an end to the "crisis," from which the "whole country suffered." [11]

In a formal sense, the Cayla Administration adhered to the policy of "decentralization," and several decrees to the effect that policies were to be determined on the "local level" were issued in the 1930's.[12] Actually, all decisions of consequence were made in the governor's office in Tananarive. The *Fokon'olona*, temporarily revived and extended from its place of origin (the central plateau), once more became inoperative. As Arbousset put it:

> The territorial chiefs who succeeded one another paid no attention to the institutions of a political and social nature that existed in the island. . . . Even under the

pretext of a most liberal policy . . . they preferred a direct administration, based on centralization. The chiefs favored the functionary, and who is the functionary if not the Merina, long acquainted with administrative practices and able to attend French schools? . . . [Thus] the Merina reimposed themselves on the other population groups as functionaries, interpreters, merchants, and settlers.[13]

In terms of economic development, the Cayla Administration had a somewhat better record. The mileage of newly built roads was doubled, from 7,200 miles in 1930, to 15,000 in 1939. Some new cash crops were introduced into the island, the port of Tamatave was improved and the city rebuilt (it had almost been destroyed by a hurricane in 1927), an agricultural credit cooperative was established (decree of April 18, 1930) along with regional advisory committees charged with the task of soil improvement and research (decree of July 17, 1933), and attempts were made to attract more private enterprise to the island by promoting the role of the chambers of commerce (decrees of November 15, 1930 and October 28, 1938) as well as that of the Banque de Madagascar. The SMOTIG was formally abolished in 1936.*

Unfortunately, the economic gains that might have brought improvements for the Malagasy were to be offset by three developments. The first was the worldwide depression, which did not bypass Madagascar either in terms of local production and exports or in the failure to attract private capital. The following table of exports is merely suggestive:

---

* However, only a few years were to pass between the abolition of the SMOTIG and the renewed drafting of labor for purposes of the "war effort."

TABLE 3

TOTAL ANNUAL EXPORTS

Year	In Metric Tons	In French Francs
1924	302,000	388,000,000
1930	181,000	370,000,000
1931	163,105	361,350,000
1932	154,830	320,070,000
1933	157,581	317,910,500
1934	168,650	345,198,000
1935	134,957	308,225,000
1936	191,566	433,298,000
1937	203,207	589,742,000

SOURCE: *Madagascar, La Grande Ile* (Paris: Agence Économique. Gouvernement Général de Madagascar, 1939), p. 39.

With the exception of rice and coffee, local production during any single year of the 1930–37 period fell below that of 1924. However, the years 1937–39 signaled a general if slow recovery. The only difficulty was that the Malagasy standard-of-living index was not considered the yardstick by which to measure economic efforts. It was rather the colonial aspect of the island's economy, buttressed by the perennial idea of the "favorable balance of trade." * And then there was World War II itself. Not only did it re-create the conditions that had existed between 1914–18 in Madagascar, but it also introduced a new factor that was to contribute to the revolt of 1947—the struggle between Vichy and Free France.

---

* The "favorable balance of trade," seen as the surplus of exports over imports, becomes an unfortunate term when applied to territories like Madagascar. There is no natural law that says that an export surplus is per se desirable. Conversely, in view of the existence of such agencies as the FIDES, and in view of the changed political-economic attitudes, a surplus of imports over exports today cannot necessarily be said to be "unfavorable." An examination of the *terms of trade* applicable to Madagascar would constitute a much more reliable method of determining the viability of the balance-of-trade situation.

5

The "Spirit of Brazzaville"

The Economic and Financial Delegations of 1924 were designed to provide representation for Malagasy as well as European interests. After a promising beginning, however, the EFD degenerated into debating societies representing no one, becoming simply another vehicle of the administrative will. The EFD was a failure—both as a political institution conceived to provide "training grounds" for eventual legislative participation in the affairs of the island and as a technical agency meant to be consulted on local budgets, taxation, loans, and agricultural and public-works projects. Thus, at the time of the defeat of the Vichy forces in the island in late 1942, there was no responsible body of Malagasy representing the population either formally or informally. In 1943, after a visit by Réné Pleven, then Commissioner for Colonies, a "mixed commission" was created by a decree of December 27, followed by another of January 22, providing for equal Malagasy-European representation.[1] There was no question of equality of representation, considering that the number of Europeans who actually lived in Madagascar did not exceed 50,000. But in theory, at least, the Malagasy members of the commission were to discuss on an

89

equal footing with the administration any matters concerning the "general interest of Madagascar." Although a host of acute and serious problems were in need of immediate attention, the mixed commission became little more than an inoperative *pro forma* body, pending the termination of the war.

The first major political reforms applicable to Madagascar were set forth at the Brazzaville Conference in 1944. Among other principles, it was established that:

> the existing consultative bodies be abolished and replaced . . . by councils of subdivision and regional councils, composed of native notables and availing themselves . . . of the framework provided by existing traditional institutions . . . by Representative Assemblies composed partly of Europeans [and] partly of natives. The members of these bodies would be elected by universal suffrage wherever and whenever . . . practicable.[2]

A Representative Council created in Madagascar by decree of March 23, 1945, was given both deliberative and consultative functions. Shortly thereafter—in October, 1946—a Representative Assembly (replacing the Council), and five provincial assemblies (composed of two sections) corresponding to the administrative provinces of Madagascar were established. The two sections became electoral colleges for the Representative Assembly, one being Malagasy by composition, the other European. Twenty-one Malagasy and fifteen Europeans were to serve in the Representative Assembly—three Europeans for each of the five provinces and four Malagasy for all provinces except Tuléar, which was alloted five seats. The thirty-six members were to be elected by the two-section majority. On the metropolitan side, the island was represented by five deputies

(two French and three Malagasy) at the French
National Assembly and eight members (two French,
six Malagasy) in the Council of the Republic. There
also ensued the abolition of the *code indigènat* by the
decrees of November 22, 1945, February 20, 1946, and
April 30, 1946, and by the *loi Lamine Guèye*.[3] By far
the most important development was the emergence
of political parties that were to set the patterns of future
political life in Madagascar. It seemed as if France had
at last moved in the right and long-overdue direction.

Four parties now appeared on the political horizon.
One was the Mouvement Démocratique de la Rénovation Malgache (MDRM). This party was organized in
Paris in February, 1946, by three Malagasy, two of whom
had been sent by constituents to Paris in December,
1945, as unofficial representatives; the other had lived in
France for many years. The first two were Dr. Raseta
and Joseph Ravoahangy, already mentioned in connection with the VVS. The third was Jacques Rabemananjara. Raseta, pardoned by Marcel Olivier, had remained
rather obscure, living in Tuléar until the end of World
War II. Ravoahangy was allowed to leave the west
coast city of Maintirano in 1935; he had taken over
the editorship of *l'Opinion*, this time in Tananarive. In
1944, Ravoahangy became President of the Agricultural
Syndicate and a year later an Assembly deputy. Jacques
Rabemananjara was a Betsimisaraka schooled by Jesuit
missionaries at Antananarivo College. Holder of a law
degree, he was also a poet, playwright, and author.
(His works include a well-received play, *Malagasy
Gods*.) He had also served in local administration and
in the Colonial Ministry for seven years. The platform
of the MDRM vacillated between two concepts.[4] One

was complete autonomy in internal affairs and a status of equality with metropolitan France within the French Union. The other was complete and immediate independence. In another respect, the two concepts represented the views of two wings within the MDRM, the "extremists" and the "moderates." The three leaders and some of their immediate associates belonged to the latter. The MDRM affiliates, Jeunesse Nationaliste (JN) and Parti Nationaliste Malgache (PANAMA), led by younger men, represented the extremist wing of the MDRM.

The MDRM was by far the best organized and the most militant of the island's four political parties and could count on a large number of sympathizers. Its only strong opponent was the Parti des Deshérités Malgaches (PADESM), formed in Madagascar in 1946, and representing a mixture of interests. Its platform called for the implementation of the Annexation Law of 1896, opposition to *Hova* hegemony in every sphere of life, and educational opportunities for non-Merina. Behind the platform of the PADESM, spelled out in its manifesto of August 6, 1946, were the "coastal interests" (limited mostly to the west coast) and the descendants of underprivileged classes, *Tsiarondahy* (royal serfs), "disinherited" (*deshérités*) by the Merina upper classes, who were the principal beneficiaries of the various French administrations. The leader of the party was himself a son of an ex-*Andevo* named Ramambason. Through its newspaper, *Voromahery (Bird of Prey)*, and its local committees, the PADESM sought to base its main appeal on socio-economic grounds directed against the privileged Merina, but not against the administration itself.

The third party was the Parti Démocratique Malgache, or PDM. The PDM was a vocal opponent of the MDRM as well as the PADESM for two different reasons. Led by Reverend Ravelojaona, it opposed the PADESM because most of its own membership came from the Merina upper classes, and the MDRM because of its extremist wing and because of the rivalry between Joseph Ravoahangy and Reverend Ravelojaona (both of whom were Merina of high birth and former members of the VVS). While also in favor of independence, the PDM did not desire it in quite the same way as did the MDRM. The PDM membership was small, but as an "intellectual" party the PDM strongly appealed to educated Merina. Its platform, expressed through the newspaper *Fandrosoamaovao* (*New Progress*), asked for a period of U.N. Trusteeship under France—a period after which independence was to be achieved. In the meantime, the PDM pledged itself to the organization of protective associations that would prevent abuse of Malagasy either by French or by other Malagasy and promised to contribute to an improvement of Malagasy economic and political life by fighting for better living standards and educational facilities as "the first preconditions of liberty." The fourth party was the Mouvement Social Malgache (MSM), a Catholic counterpart of the PDM, with a very similar platform for the "safeguarding of liberties" and eventual self-government qualified by "eternal justice." Its membership was extremely small. The MSM opposed both the PDM and the MDRM but not the PADESM.

The provincial elections of 1946 went heavily in favor of the MDRM. Of the sixty-two members in the first electoral college, the "conservative" Europeans defeated the "liberals" by a three-to-one margin. In the provinces of Tananarive and Tamatave, all of the thirty-six seats went to members of the MDRM. In Tuléar Province, the MDRM won thirteen out of twenty seats; in Majunga Province, five out of eighteen; and in the province of Fianarantsoa, ten out of eighteen. Considering that, in the provincial assemblies, the MDRM won sixty-four out of ninety-two seats in the second electoral college, its victory in the Representative Assembly should have been assured. But this was not to be the case. With a two-section majority vote, the PADESM obtained twelve seats to the MDRM's nine. Of the six deputies for the Council of the Republic, three were members of the PADESM and three of the MDRM (Ranaivo, Raberivelo, and Bezara). Only in the Paris Assembly did the MDRM get all of the three seats (Rabemananjara, Ravoahangy, and Raseta). The Representative Assembly did not meet until 1947.

6

The Revolt of 1947

About midnight on March 29–30, 1947, outbreaks of violence started in various parts of the island. At Maromanga, the insurgents attacked and inflicted heavy losses upon a French army garrison. Manakara fell into rebel hands after hand-to-hand combat with a strong police force. Communications between Amilobé and Diego-Suarez were cut. Police stations were attacked at Vohipeno and Farafangana. With the exception of the city proper, the French lost the entire Mananjary region. The same pattern was followed in Ambila, Anjiro, and Anosibé. One of the strongest military outposts in Madagascar, located some 118 miles northeast of Tananarive, was completely isolated from the rest of the island. In many sections of the northeast and southeast, European settlers were beaten, and some were killed. Hundreds of pro-French Malagasy and converts to Christianity were tortured and murdered. Some churches and missions were razed. By June–July, 1947, the backbone of the revolt was crushed. It was not, however, until the end of 1948 that the last rebel pockets were wiped out in the forests of Madagascar.[1]

The exact number of Malagasy who perished in the

revolt has never been determined. The reprisals by the administration and the army were swift and often brutal. An entire trainload of prisoners was massacred near Maromanga. Many rebels incarcerated in the prisons of Farafangana, Manakara, and Mananjary were executed in the courtyards without trial. The same happened on a larger scale in the rural areas. There were heavy losses in the city of Fianarantsoa, too. This city had 21,000 residents in 1941, and only 19,000 in 1950. At the same time, however, the province of Fianarantsoa attracted a considerable number of immigrants. Its population in 1939–40 did not exceed 850,000. At present, the figure is close to 1.5 million. But there is little doubt that the population decline in the city itself was due to the revolt. In the rural districts affected most by the revolt, ancient tribal vendettas added to the bloodshed. To some extent, the rivalries between militant political (PADESM-MDRM) factions were translated into acts of physical violence. The most extreme estimate put the death toll at 90,000.[2] In 1948, the administration estimated the number of dead or presumed dead at 60,000–80,000.[3] Two years later, an administration document giving a "detailed breakdown" of the losses put the number of victims at only 11,342: 140 French, 2 Indians, 19 Chinese, 2 Syrians, 17 Senegalese, and 1,646 Malagasy killed by the rebel forces; 4,126 Malagasy killed by government forces; and 5,390 presumed to have died in the forests, mostly of cold and starvation. Considering the sources, it would be difficult to regard either the low or high casualty figures as accurate. There is also a wide discrepancy between the administration's 1948 estimate and its 1950 report. Furthermore, the question of timing is important. In 1948, with the revolt barely over, the administration would be less likely to deflate the figure. Moreover, in 1950, the dignitaries and elders who were asked to report those missing to district chiefs were hardly disposed to spell out the whole truth. A high number of missing would seem to indicate that the entire village had supported the revolt. Consequently, those districts not generally affected may have reported accurate figures (roughly two thirds of the island was relatively or completely unaffected), while those in the main areas of revolt probably reported a much lower number of missing. An estimate of 60,000 is still only an estimate, yet because of the reasons enumerated it would seem closer to the true figure than either 90,000 or 11,000.

The question immediately poses itself: Who were the rebels and why did they revolt? The intensity that marked the initial stages of the revolt, the brutality on both sides, and the loss of about 1 per cent of the total population of the island might lead to the obvious conclusion that the five decades of French presence in Madagascar had had only negative effects. Such a conclusion, however, would not only be facile but also wrong.

Under French rule, Madagascar became more advanced than most of the European possessions in Africa south of the Sahara. Madagascar's 35–40 per cent literacy rate compared favorably with that of the Belgian Congo. Per-capita public and private educational facilities (including the number of students) in Madagascar in 1946 exceeded those in French West Africa by more than 50 per cent.* No institution comparable to the Academie Malgache (which, by 1946, had 300 Malagasy and European members and had published more than 100 books) could be found in sub-Saharan Africa. The three main killers of the Malagasy—malaria, leprosy, and syphilis—were brought under control and the death rate was steadily declining.

Many freedoms existing in France, it is true, were not allowed in Madagascar, while some privileges granted to the Malagasy in theory were meaningless in practice. On the other hand, some freedoms that had not existed under Merina rule or under tribal systems were introduced and preserved. To put it in another, if slightly unfashionable, way, the replacement of the Merina colonial administration by its French counterpart did not, so far as quite a few Malagasy were concerned, represent a great tragedy. Slavery, once a firmly entrenched institution, was never revived. There was exploitation of the Malagasy under the SMOTIG regime and within the sharecropping (*métayage*) system, but any attempt to equate these with slavery cannot be considered even remotely objective. Although the new approach of Africanist historians reflects the trend among African intellectuals to minimize precolonial

---

* In 1950, there were approximately 5,700 Protestant missions and schools and 803,575 Protestants in Madagascar. Protestant religious personnel numbered about 4,000; the number of pupils was 47,000. In 1955, the number of Protestants was given at 827,000. There were 8 Catholic vicarates, 3 apostolic prefectures, and about 800,000 Catholics in 1950. The total number of Catholic religious personnel was 6,777. The actual number of Catholic missions and schools is not available, but about 75,000 children attended Catholic schools. In 1955, there were about 923,000 Catholics. Reports for that year put the number of practicing Muslims at 100,000. See *L'oeuvre des missions protestantes a Madagascar*, and *Les missions catholiques à Madagascar* (Paris, Cahiers Charles de Foucauld), pp. 309–39. The *Bulletin de Madagascar*, No. 162, November, 1959, contains the most recent data.

intertribal warfare, it cannot be denied that it did exist, and that the establishment of colonial or central authority prevented its reoccurrence.

As for the *"colon* problem"—confined to some areas of the east coast—it was never uniform in intensity. The periodic scarcity of indigenous labor had forced many a settler of European stock to be far less colonial-minded than his white confreres in Algeria, Kenya, Southern Rhodesia, or South Africa. The *petit blanc,* or "white-trash," elements were concentrated in one or two cities, but their particular brand of poison was offset by the egalitarian attitude of other whites. The color bar, where it existed, was much more a matter of individual than of collective practice. Intermarriages between Europeans and Malagasy were not uncommon. The army units stationed in Madagascar on the whole kept a good record during the five decades that preceded the revolt. In spite of *mercantilisme* in Paris and a colonial economy in Madagascar, it cannot be said that no economic benefits accrued to the Malagasy, or that economic exploitation was the only hallmark of French rule. If, as economists acknowledge, urbanization is one method of determining the "rate of progress," then Madagascar compares favorably to the former AOF-AEF countries. About 13 per cent of the Malagasy live in towns and cities of more than 2,000, as compared to 9.4 per cent in the former AOF-AEF areas. Only a few thousand Malagasy have become well-to-do, and perhaps no more than two or three hundred persons in the agricultural sector, which, according to 1958 statistics, houses about 87 per cent of the population, have become fairly rich. But there are several hundred thousand farmers cultivating commercial crops on their own, and often they manage to earn a good living.

Although, in comparison with most of French-speaking Africa south of the Sahara, the Malagasy emerge as having been relatively well off, the record in absolute terms was not nearly as good. Somewhat less than 47 per cent of all children between the ages of five and fifteen could attend school. Few of those excluded from minimum education were Merina. According to official sources in 1951, French agricultural concessions amounted to 1,478,142 hectares; 553,787 hectares of forest lands were being exploited; and more than 0.5 million hectares became the property of mining concerns for the purposes of research, development, and exploitation.[4] It should be added that of the French agricultural concessions, less than one third were under actual cultivation, while most of them were in the most fertile areas of the island. Thus the many Malagasy in subsistence farming (and that means close to 50 per cent of the population) were unable to farm almost a million idle hectares of the best land. The million or so hectares for mining concessions included coal (principally the Sakoa fields) and known oil deposits that were never developed. From the timber exploitations the Malagasy obtained almost no benefits. Between 1945 and 1950, the net income of the eight largest French corporations alone amounted to about 6.08 billion francs. The salaries of professional Malagasy were scandalously low in comparison with those of Europeans in the same professions. Although the foregoing discussion of the pluses and minuses of the history of French presence in Madagascar has not been exhaustive, still it must be obvious that the 1947 revolt

was bound to come as a shock to Paris.* The surprise
of the French was indeed so great that they almost
came to believe the simplistic explanation proffered in
the first reports from Madagascar that the revolt had
been started by Communists, although their influence
was almost nonexistent. It was not until August, 1947,
almost six months after the beginning of the revolt,
that a more realistic, although still inadequate, explanation was advanced. In his speech before the first meeting of the Representative Assembly, High Commissioner Coppet (1946–48) accused the MDRM of having
been the actual organizer of the revolt. He qualified
the charge by adding that the success of the "extreme
nationalists" was made possible only because they were
able to exploit several legitimate grievances of the local
population—grievances that "could be traced to the
last war." The Vichy Administration, according to Coppet, had completely disregarded local economic and
social problems. Production decreases, loss of trade,[5]
black market, forced labor, and the abuses of and mis-
management by the bureaus of Rice Distribution and
Deforestation had compounded the problems of the
Malagasy. The "quota system" instituted by the Bureau
of Rice Distribution was responsible for the confisca-
tion of large quantities of rice from thousands of Malagasy farmers, thus leaving them without staple food, in
addition to other hardships they had to face during the
war. The end of hostilities in 1942 in Madagascar did
not automatically end the abuses of the Bureau; they
continued for another two years. The fact that most
Malagasy could not distinguish between two different

* See Jacques Rabemananjara's discussion in *"Presence Africaine,"*
Nationalisme et Problèmes Malgaches (Paris, 1958), pp. 15–48.

French governments was hardly helpful. The fighting in 1942 between the British and Free French on the one hand, and the Vichy forces on the other, had destroyed the image of "white infallibility." [6] The presence of some 15,000 veterans of World War II, who had returned to Madagascar from overseas service with the Free French army, provided the insurgents with a willing and combat-ready cadre for the revolt. This point was underscored by Coppet, when he said that: "unhappy with their lot, incapable of readjusting to conditions of normal work, they furnished an important contribution to the perpetrators of the disorders." [7] Coppet was only touching upon the deeper truth, and self-serving statements attempting to put the bulk of the blame on the war, on Vichy, the MDRM, and the *deraciné,* or uprooted, Malagasy war veterans did much to undo some of the positive accomplishments of the past. Another and far more interesting attempt to explain the causes of the revolt came two years later from the pen of an astute French scholar, Dr. O. Mannoni, who was also the Director of the administration's General Information Department. In his *Psychologie de le Colonisation,*[8] Dr. Mannoni sought to explain the revolt in terms of Malagasy psychology and the reaction to colonial rule. Using the complex of dependence as the pillar of his analysis, he contended that the postwar freedoms frightened the Malagasy and that, hence, they revolted—not because they wanted independence, but because they wanted a reassertion of authority. Dr. Mannoni's book is a fascinating mixture of psychological analysis, erudition, and penetrating thinking. His conclusion, however, is not very original. A similar argument, namely, that freedom without

adequate preparation leads to irresponsibility and excess, was advanced cogently before Mannoni—and since
—on nonpsychological grounds. The argument has its
merits, but in the case of Madagascar it has as yet to
be proved. There are other, much simpler, and de-
monstrable explanations of the revolt.

The root of the trouble may perhaps be found in
the disappearance of the type of administrator who, like
Gallieni, had a sense of dual loyalty and who—while
not entirely faultless—spared no effort to delve into
history, to understand the nature of local problems, to
guide social change rather than to create or repress it.
In his stead came the era of the bureaucratic machine
with its narcissism and self-importance (strengthened
by the Merina functionaries' propensity for procedure),
unwilling and unable to understand. It is this machine
that had built a state within a state, with its own laws
and coterie, divorced from Paris as well as from the
Malagasy, reacting to nonconformity much as had the
feudal Merina Kingdom of Ranavalona I, and buttressed by the *colon* and the corporation. Neither
Cayla's first administration (1930–39), nor the succeed-
ing administrations of Coppet (1939–40), Cayla (1940–
41), Anet (1941–42), and Saint-Mart (1943–46) had a
concept of responsibility transcending the narrow interests of the machine. The social change, marked by de-
tribalization—begun by Gallieni, revived temporarily by
Olivier—and manifesting itself on the political level in
the nationalist movement of the 1920's, underwent two
decades of regression not so much by design as through
sheer ignorance and inertia.

Although the defeat of Vichy brought a new governor
in 1943, the same self-perpetuating hierarchy saw to it

that the problems tackled would be the problems of the machine, the corporation, and the settler—not the problems of the Malagasy. Regimes changed, but not the outlook. The abuses of World War I were simply repeated during World War II, and once again thousands of Malagasy were fighting overseas on the side of France. In Madagascar itself there were "natives" who were able to differentiate between Vichy and Free France. Among them, for example, was the daughter of Jules Ranaivo, who became the first woman to join the Free French Forces in 1942, and who was executed in the Moramanga prison courtyard by a firing squad "loyal" to the Fourth Republic. Then, in late 1944, a new France met in Brazzaville, setting forth long-overdue reforms that were incorporated into the Malagasy Charter in 1945. It was not until November, 1945, and June, 1946, that the reforms were made fully operative in so far as parties, elections, and formal parliamentary structures were concerned. The thinking in Brazzaville, conditioned by colonial contributions to Free France as well as by De Gaulle and Felix Eboué, had fired the imagination of the Malagasy. Far from being afraid of new freedoms or from seeking to "escape" from them, they had a very mundane sense of appreciation.

> We can at last rejoice in the precious gift the Government and the Parliament of France have accorded us. The *code indigènat* is finally abolished. Forced labor in all its forms has been done away with. Finally, colonialism itself is dead, for we are no longer subjects. The *loi Lamine Guèye* has made us citizens. . . . Everyone is now [equal] under the laws of France.[9]

It was not the Brazzaville thinking that lagged far behind the desires of the fairly competent Malagasy elite. It was rather the local administration that was completely out of step with Brazzaville. The oft-repeated statement that France's colonial reforms granted "too little, too late" overlooks the simple truth that France is not a monolithic state, and that between France and colonial capitals like Tananarive the distance was much greater than a few thousand miles of land and ocean. The emergence of extremist nationalistic tendencies in prerevolt Madagascar need not be traced to the psychological complex of dependence or to the war veterans. The expectations, lifted high in Brazzaville, were completely frustrated in Tananarive. To quote Mannoni himself, "Half the Europeans encouraged the Malagasy to do as he pleased as a free man; the other half were more hostile to him than before—their hostility being the psychological counterpart of the paternalistic attitude." While the suppression of the VVS or of the movement of the 1920's (moderate as it was) could hardly have been called "paternalism" (a good father would allow his children at least some liberties), Mannoni's contention can be documented. The Representative Assembly did not convene until more than two weeks after the revolt had begun. Nor was the Assembly "representative" in the strict sense of the word. The MDRM, as a party that had won the majority of popular votes and seats in the provincial assemblies, was not given its rightful share of seats in the main Assembly, because the local administration unabashedly used the built-in advantages of the dual electoral-college system to minimize the power of the

MDRM and maximize that of the PADESM, which it strongly favored and supported. Nor is it true, as has been alleged, that the PADESM was nothing more than an administrative creation. The administration simply found it useful to support a party proposing the programs of 1929 in 1946.

True to its traditional nature, the administration could not bring itself to communicate, even on an unequal level, with the Political Bureau of the MDRM. Even if allowance is made for the fact that a "colonial-minded" administration could not adjust fully to the spirit of the Brazzaville reforms by accepting a non-conformist elite as a legal and political partner, there were other means by which it could have reduced the possibility of violence. Signs of unrest and dissatisfaction during the entire year prior to the revolt were not lacking. Instead of communicating with the leadership of the MDRM, the administration opted for arrests and fines of individuals, neglecting completely the obvious alternative of *détente* by negotiation. In this connection it is only pertinent to say that High Commissioner Coppet complained that nothing could be done against the party because of laws promulgated outside the island that protected parties in general, and that hence only individual "transgressors" could be "punished." [10]

Something else must be added, too. A revolt requires organization and preparation. The local police officials were constantly warned of possible large-scale violence by their own agents and by opponents of the MDRM. On March 18, 1947, M. Vincent-Dolor, the chief administrator of Fianarantsoa Province, sent the following telegram to his district heads:

According to information given me in confidence by the military authorities, certain Malagasy are about to launch a revolt against Frenchmen on March 29, beginning with Tananarive. Take measures to alert all posts to prepare for any eventuality.[11]

Passions on both sides, of course, ran high and rumors were rife, but Vincent-Dolor took the precaution of going to Tananarive to report to the High Commissioner's office the following day. On March 25, he sent another telegram to that office:

I hereby confirm the information given during the conference of administrative chiefs of provinces, according to which information—obtained from a commander of the southern subdivision—an action against the Europeans would be unleashed on March 29 in the territory. Although these rumors, which occur at regular intervals and which constitute a war of nerves, should not be accorded more than relative importance, I have thought it wise to advise discreetly the taking of precautions in the whole of the province.[12]

This and similar evidence has been used to prove that the local administration deliberately sought to provoke the revolt. The charge would be hard to sustain. The Brazzaville reforms had put the local administration on notice, and the mood in Paris left little doubt that the last thing the administration wanted to have on its hands was a major revolt. While little credence can be given to the charge that the revolt was "provoked," there can be no dispute about the fact that nothing was done to prevent it. Once again, the Malagasy were underestimated, both as human beings and as a force to be reckoned with.

If the question of why the revolt took place requires

more than pat or partisan answers, the task of discovering its planners cannot be fulfilled by simply pointing to the leaders of the MDRM. No amount of post-revolt polemics can refute the fact that the party's top leadership *knew* of the preparations for the revolt. Yet at the same time, the principal masterminds of the revolt were men considerably younger than the three top MDRM leaders, close to the semisecret and militant PANAMA and JN, whose leaders were reported to be Rakotondrabe, Betrevola, and Ravelonahina. The Political Bureau of the MDRM was itself split between the younger, more activist members like Tata Max and its Secretary-General, Rabeantoandro, and the older and more moderate men like Dr. Raherivelo. In a sense, the three leaders were faced with a difficult situation, one not without analogy and likely to repeat itself elsewhere, although perhaps less tragically. It is a situation in which the human element comes to the fore in that the younger men challenge the established leaders, more often than not successfully.

> Do you think, you other deputies, that we are going to leave you in peace? . . . The people suffer quite enough as it is. With your French Union the people will have ample time to perish from misery. No, we have no more time to wait. Youth, which despises your policies of procrastination and irresolution, is moving away from the MDRM. We want action; it's time to go into action.[13]

Furthermore, none of the chiefs of the MDRM could betray a compatriot by denouncing him to the police or the military. Following the outbreak of hostilities, Dr. Raseta, Joseph Ravoahangy, and Jacques Rabemananjara dissociated themselves from the rebels. Ravoa-

hangy and Rabemananjara, who were present in Madagascar during the revolt, blamed each other for allowing
the event to take place. On the other hand, Martin
Rakotovao, Adjunct Secretary of the party, blamed Dr.
Raseta, who was then in Paris.

Much has been written, both con and pro, about the
three deputies, but their individual and collective roles
in the revolt cannot be properly evaluated on the
strength of their own statements about the only three
concrete facts that have emerged from the event: the
meeting of the Political Bureau on March 27, 1947; a
telegram sent on the same date to all branches of the
MDRM; and the simultaneous outbreaks marking the
beginning of the revolt during the night of March
29–30. Twenty members of the Political Bureau, including Ravoahangy and Rabemananjara, met in
Tananarive at noon on March 27 to discuss the political
tensions on the island and what to do about them. The
result of the meeting was a telegram written in French
by Rabemananjara and translated into Malagasy by
Ravoahangy, following an agreement between them
that the situation was critical and that, given extreme
reactions on both the administration and JN-PANAMA
sides, they must act to prevent violence. Moreover, both
agreed that the party had little to gain from open
clashes and sought insurance against reprisals. The
telegram, signed by Raseta, Ravoahangy, Rabemananjara, and the Political Bureau, ordered all members of
the MDRM "to keep calm and composed in the face
of all maneuvers and provocations designed to arouse
disturbances among the Malagasy people and to sabotage
the peaceful policies of the MDRM." [14]

When the revolt broke out forty-eight hours later,

the administration claimed that the telegram was a "prearranged signal" for the revolt. Subsequently, at the Tananarive trials, Prosecutor Lucciardi called the telegram irrefutable proof that the top MDRM leadership had masterminded the uprising. Judging from their own statements, a conflict of personalities existed between Ravoahangy and Rabemananjara. Ravoahangy, who had practically fathered the nationalist movement, was an old in-fighter for whom politics, and hence the "art of the possible," was a way of life. Rabemananjara, a sensitive artist and intellectual, although a member of the new generation that was more French than the French themselves, was unwilling to allow his feelings for the best in French culture to interfere with his judgments concerning the future of his people. Because the "politician" and the "intellectual" did not get along too well, they were prone to accuse each other of "duplicity" in connection with the actual meaning of the telegram, and thus inadvertently they accepted the administration's charge that the telegram signaled the revolt. Yet there is positive proof that the administration was forewarned of the exact date at least twelve days in advance, and nine days before the telegram itself was composed and sent to all branches of the MDRM. This is as far as the present inquiry can be carried; the reader will have to arrive at his own conclusion. Two further qualifications need to be made.

In approaching the 1947 revolt as a subject of study having implications beyond the event itself, the first thing to be noted is that a full and truly objective report has as yet to be written. More than a decade has passed since that tragic happening, but all of the

French-language literature concerning it remains hope-
lessly bogged down amid the conflicting partisanship
of armchair liberals or of those who for one reason or
another support the local administration's point of
view, or even that of Communists and crypto-Commu-
nists. Each group applies the same "rational method"
to attribute some degree of guilt to either the
nationalists or to the French administration. English-
language literature on the subject is scant and unreveal-
ing. The second qualification that need be made is in
what light to regard the revolt itself. The tragedy of the
uprising lies in the loss of human life and the punishment meted out to those directly or indirectly connected
with it. The end of hostilities brought a whole series
of trials in its wake. Raseta and Ravoahangy were
sentenced to death, and Rabemananjara received a life
sentence.* At the end of the trials, between 5,000 and
6,000 individuals received penalties ranging from
eighteen months in prison to death. The number of
those executed is not known. Raseta and Ravoahangy
were saved from execution by the combined pressure of
the French press, private groups of citizens, and many
members of the French Parliament. Ultimately,
Rabemananjara's and their sentences were commuted,
and they were exiled to France until 1963, and granted
freedom of movement within the country. Raseta spent
most of his time in Cannes; Ravoahangy, in Toulouse;

---

* Rabemananjara was arrested on April 12, 1947, and interrogated
under extreme duress *prior* to the suspension of his parliamentary immunity. He was released only because the National Assembly in Paris
requested his presence. His stirring report to the Assembly (*NED*, No.
714, August 30, 1947, pp. 25–31) should be required reading for all
those who wish to study the revolt.

Rabemananjara, in Paris. All three kept in touch with their homeland and continued to represent a significant body of Malagasy nationalists.

The revolt did, however, have one major, salutary effect. In the 1950's, Paris could no longer remain complacent, and Tananarive had to realize that the time in which it could still "carry on as usual" was at best limited. A liberal and democratic France could ill afford to continue for long to be represented in Madagascar by an archaic antithesis of itself. As Alfred Sauvy put it in 1952,

> Enmeshed in its own internal difficulties and trials, France did not always find the time to give Madagascar the attention it rightly deserved. Involved in dramatic events, men like Gallieni could not lift their voices, as they would have done under other circumstances, to prevent the Great Isle from being forgotten. . . . As painful as they are, the events of 1947 have had the percussive role of innovation. And it is certainly a new period, at the same time more difficult and more fruitful, that seems to have come into being.[15]

III

MADAGASCAR AND FRANCE:

THE NEW PHASE—1948–60

Reflections on the Economy

From 1948 until the passing of the *loi cadre* (enabling act) in June, 1956, the regrouping of nationalist forces in Madagascar was overshadowed by activities in the social and economic realms. The eight years of relative political lull could too easily be explained as having been the product of the 1947–48 experience. A state of martial law continued to exist after the revolt. The memory of this violent interlude was still fresh in the island, and neither the politically conscious Malagasy nor the local French administration could be expected to duplicate the tensions of 1946. Actually, underneath the *détente* there were some significant developments. Four years after the revolt, in June, 1951, one of the few survivors of the younger MDRM leaders won a local election, in spite of the efforts of the administration in alliance with the conservative European and Malagasy elements to rig the elections. Several strikes took place between 1951–53, heralding another important development. These were, however, nothing more than harbingers of a regrouping of forces. Another change was that, for the first time, the local hierarchy and its new head, Pierre de Chevigné, did not share the same outlook. Coincidental was the fact that Paris became increasingly aware that something must be done for the island's economy on a fairly large scale and in a different way than had hitherto been the case if renewed extremism were to be avoided. After a hesitant start, economic efforts gained momentum by 1952—a date that also brought about new labor legislation for the overseas territories of France.

With the visit to Madagascar by Gaston Deferre and the introduction of the *loi cadre*, which he helped draft, political activities became overt and took marked precedence over all other spheres of endeavor. Thus it may be said that the postrevolt period can be divided into two parts: the period of economic activity with relatively weak signs of political life (1949–56), and the period of rapid political development (1956–60) leading first to the creation of the Malagasy Republic and, ultimately, to its independence.

Agriculture—after sixty years of French presence in Madagascar—continues to be the pillar of the island's economy. As of January, 1956, the working population of the island was given as 1.06 million.[1] Only 8 per cent of the working population were engaged in fields other than agriculture.[2] (These 8 per cent, however, did include 70,000 wage earners in the agricultural sector. This category is not cited in the table below.)
In 1958, the total figure increased to 166,000, the greatest increase taking place in the categories of domestic servants and professions.

The vast majority of Malagasy are engaged in small-scale farming. Maurice Rossin, until recently Director of Agriculture at the Ministry for Overseas France,

TABLE 4

Economic Sector	Number of Employees
Public Administration and technical services	38,471
Forestry	8,057
Mining	6,034
Industry	19,479
Construction and public works	18,240
Transport and maintenance	12,067
Commerce and professions	22,553
Domestic servants	32,214
Grand Total	157,115

notes that in January, 1957, about 87 per cent of the Malagasy lived in rural communities of less than 2,000. In addition, a number of Malagasy who live in towns contribute a considerable number of man-hours to agriculture. In 1958, there were 37 towns of 2,000–5,000; 10 towns of 5,000–20,000; 5 towns of 20,000–100,000, and one city of more than 100,000. The total population of 53 towns was 554,063.

In any discussion of present-day Malagasy agriculture, several features should be singled out. The first is diversification. From the point of view of local consumption this is important, not only because diversification makes a mixed diet possible, but, more important, because it reduces hardship among those who depend on a single crop both for income and consumption. Rice is the one crop that must be available in quantities sufficient to meet the basic demand of the Malagasy people, estimated at approximately 240 lbs. per capita annually. With the exception of Burma, Madagascar is said to be the world's largest per-capita consumer of rice. The average 1957 consumption is given at 330 lbs. per capita. The following are some of the facts that serve to illustrate the diversity of Malagasy agriculture:

a. Although three principal crops occupy almost 80 per cent of the total land under cultivation, none of the other produce—except corn and yams—occupies more than 40,000 hectares of the remaining 20 per cent of the total.[3] The three main crops are rice, coffee and cassava. Each occupies a different place in the Malagasy economy.

b. In terms of its economic development, Madagascar resembles tropical Africa in that it is composed of a group of productive "islands" or "pockets" in varying stages of progress. In many cases, natural barriers exist between these "islands," the removal of which would not always justify the cost.

c. Climatic conditions are not uniform throughout the island.[4]

The increasing amount of agricultural produce that, since the 1950's, has been consumed locally, either directly by the producer himself or indirectly through the local market places, constitutes a second important trend. Rice, cassava, corn, potatoes, kidney beans, yams, and other types of produce are rarely channeled into export. This statement, however, needs clarification. In 1924, for instance, rice exports amounted to over 80,000 tons against an annual production of 650,000 tons, or 12.3 per cent of the total rice produced that year. In addition, the mid-1920's were a boom period, reaching a level hitherto unknown in Madagascar. The picture changed considerably during the first half of the present decade, as can be seen from the figures given below:

TABLE 5

Year	Production (in tons)	Export (in tons)
1951	816,000	24,600
1952	1,022,000	40,600
1953	1,050,000	45,000
1954	1,050,000	14,900
1955	1,150,000	44,700
1956	1,100,000	36,000
1957	1,220,000	(not available)

During the 1951–56 period, the average amount of rice exported was 3.4 per cent of the total production. With the exception of 1953, the export of rice during this period never exceeded 4 per cent of the total production.

In 1938, for example, the export of cassava and its derivatives represented over 6 per cent of the total cash value of all exports. In 1956, the export of cassava had fallen below 2 per cent of the total. In terms of tonnage, 29,600 tons left Madagascar in 1938, as against only 4,600 in 1956. The total amount of land alloted to the cultivation of cassava has remained almost unchanged (180,000 hectares) during the last ten years. It should be noted that tapioca accounted for one third of the 1938 cassava tonnage exported, while in 1956, it accounted for 95 per cent, pointing to increasing local consumption of cassava and, to a lesser degree, of tapioca. Much the same can be said for corn, the export of which decreased from 54,000 tons in 1938, to 2,700 tons in 1956, without a similar drop in annual production. (In 1938, the total production of corn was given at 82,000 tons, and in 1956 at 68,000 tons.)

Thus it can be seen that rice, cassava, and corn—especially rice—formerly mixed consumption-export products, have become predominantly local-consumption crops. To put it differently, the population of Madagascar was better fed in the 1951–57 period than at any time before. On the other hand, the decrease in these exports and the increasing rice production and consumption also reflect the fact that for the first time in the known history of Madagascar the net gain in births over deaths has surpassed 100,000. This is quite significant if it is recalled that the net population gain in 1946 was 9,200, as compared to the net population gain of 105,800 in 1956. There are further indications that by the end of 1960, the population of Madagascar may exceed 5.4 million.

Coffee is another major crop. Unlike the three crops already discussed, coffee is a cash crop earmarked almost exclusively for export. This is evidenced by the fact that coffee, which occupies only about 12 per cent of the total cultivated area, accounted for over 43 per cent of the total cash value of exports in 1956. Coffee production has been increasing without interruption since the end of the last war. In 1946, for example, only 17,000 tons of coffee were produced in Madagascar. In 1956, the total production exceeded 52,000 tons. It is estimated, overoptimistically perhaps, that over 75,000 tons of coffee will have been produced in 1960.

Another agricultural problem that should be singled out is "primitive farming," which still seems to be widely practiced and involves the use of crude artifacts as well as the slash-and-burn technique—*tavy*—with a corresponding land wastage and poor utilization of man power. *Tavy* is an aspect of the Malagasy economy resistant to change. Although some inroads have been made in the past, the administrative approach to the problem has generally been legalistic, sometimes harsh (as in the case of the Tanala—an area heavily involved in the revolt of 1947), and mostly ineffective. About the only way in which *tavy* will give way to new methods of cultivation is through direct education (by government agricultural experts) and imitation (infusion of better farming techniques into areas where *tavy* is widespread, as in the Tanala-Betsileo country).

In the field of agriculture, the years immediately following World War II were devoted largely to the study of modernization. The gain in population in recent years has not in itself been sufficient to alleviate the lack of effective man power, while consumption continues to rise. As in the former Belgian Congo, modernization of agriculture is seen in Madagascar as the best possible solution to this problem. The first postwar study in relation to the improvement and modernization of agriculture was conducted by a mixed French-Malagasy commission created in December, 1943. Its recommendations were later embodied in a decree (November, 1944), but no action was taken until 1948–49. Instead it was decided that another, less general, study should be undertaken. The result was the establishment of experimental group projects in each of the administrative provinces of the island. The success or failure of these *collectivités témoins* was to determine the applicability of what the French called a "simple, efficient, and realistic" approach. Prior to the final evaluation of these pilot projects, the Ministry for France Overseas in Paris had decided to introduce a new rural policy into Madagascar, one already applied in North Africa, by ordering the establishment of Secteurs Expérimentaux de Modernisation Rurale (SEMR) later renamed Zones de Développement. It should be mentioned that the French regarded the pilot projects as extensions of the ancient *Fokon'olona,* while the SEMR constituted the panoply of a modern state. In June, 1950, the *collectivités témoins* were superseded by the more permanent Collectivés Autochtones Rurales Modernisées, referred to as the CRAM.

Although there are over two dozen CRAM's in Madagascar, it would be difficult to say as yet anything more than that their economic success is limited. In the first place, they have been successful only in those areas designated as experimental sectors for rural modernization (SEMR), such as the areas of Mahavavy-Sambirano, Basse-Betsiboka, Morondava, Lake Alaotra, Pangalanes, Mandrare, and Mangoky-Sakoa.[5] This is not to be interpreted as an aspect of the power struggle between the Paris ministry and the administrators in Madagascar in the sense that, by coincidence, progress is being made only in those areas in which both Paris and Tananarive have a direct hand. The "coincidence" is due mainly to the economic-geographic fact that the pattern of large-scale agricultural development is still "islandic," as pointed out earlier, and that such improvements as have been made took place after 1950, and also in the regions with higher productivity. In the second place, the most important and beneficial function of CRAM is that it made possible a rational distribution and application of the loans and grants pumped into the Malagasy economy by France through the general development fund—Fonds d'Investissement pour le Développement Économique et Sociale des Territoires d'Outre-Mer (FIDES). Although there have been periods in which the French have sought to help "equally" all those "eligible" for assistance, and although local desiderata were fairly well represented through the twelve *chambres de commerce, d'industrie et d'agriculture,* the implementation of "equal assistance has tended to work in favor of only a few Europeans and Malagasy, and it has worked better in commerce and the processing industry than in agriculture. The CRAM's, therefore, have broadened "equal assistance" in agriculture. Their success in this respect can be deduced from the recent proposal (August, 1957) of certain Europeans and Malagasy, submitted to the then Vice-President of the Conseil de Gouvernement, Philibert Tsiranana, for the establishment of separate chambers of agriculture. (A contrary view is held by the former Secretary-General of Madagascar, M. Joudain, who maintained that separate chambers of agriculture would "benefit primarily the small Malagasy farmer.")

The fact that the CRAM's made possible a more rational allotment of funds for the improvement and modernization of agriculture does not mean, as yet, that they have been fully utilized. They do not obtain funds

directly from FIDES, but indirectly through an intermediary agency, the Central Fund, or Caisse Centrale
d'Équipement Agricole et de Modernisation du Paysanat, whose function it is to coordinate provincial
budgets and FIDES aid, and allot money where "most
needed." The Central Fund is under the control of
a political body (Conseil Supérieur du Paysanat) in
which the provincial delegates frequently have the
decisive word, not only on how budgets of their own
provinces should be coordinated, but also on the distribution of FIDES loans and grants. This has resulted
in a situation whereby the most productive sectors of
the Malagasy economy receive most of the funds.
Although this system at present fits rather well into
the islandic pattern of development, the local government may find it necessary in the near future to turn
its attention to the less-developed parts of Madagascar
rather than continue the improvement of only those
areas already in the productive stage. The error of the
1920's and 1930's is being repeated, although some new
areas have been added and although the Malagasy
themselves now have a major voice in the matter.

Under the ten-year development plan officially sanc-
tioned in 1949, between 45 billion and 57 billion francs
were to be spent in three successive stages. The first
stage (1949–51) was to be devoted to the replacement
of obsolete and worn-out equipment, some technical
assistance, soil study and some administrative improvements. The total expenditure envisaged for the first
stage was in the amount of 12 billion francs. The second
stage (1952–56) [6] was to be more extensive and more
balanced, as shown below.[7]

TABLE 6

Production sector	Planned Expenditures (in billions of francs)
Improvement studies	.400
Direct agricultural production	.525
Soil improvement, reclamation, and flood control	2.750
Forests	.380
Cattle breeding (animal husbandry)	1.330
	5.385
Equipment	
Railroads	.960
Roads and bridges	1.400
Ports	2.230
Navigable rivers and canals	.600
Air transport	.770
Communications	.597
	6.557
Social development	
Public health	1.350
Education	.955
Urban housing	.450
Urban and rural works	.360
	3.115
Grand Total	15.057

By far the largest item (2.75 billion francs) is earmarked for "soil improvement, reclamation, and flood control." Of the 2.75 billion francs alloted under this item, 1.25 billion was to go to the single region of Lake Alaotra. Because of this regional stress and because Alaotra is the most advanced of the seven development

zones, a good idea can be gained regarding the islandic
development of Madagascar by a brief but detailed
examination of projected Alaotra works within the
1952–56 stage of the ten-year plan.

In the Ambatondrazaka sector, 5,000 hectares are at
present being cultivated by traditional methods. An
additional 1,500 hectares are considered cultivable.
Most of the improvements, which will include flood
control, drainage, and irrigation works covering both
the cultivated and cultivable land, are still in the
project stage. The flood waters are to be sent toward
the Sahabe River and Lake, through a system of diver-
sion canals merging into a collecting canal, which is
to have an average width of 1,300 feet. Surface drainage
is to be directed toward the Amparihilava Depression.
A network of irrigation embarkments will complete the
project. The entire cost is estimated at 120 million
francs CFA, and the project is to be completed by 1963.

The sector, which includes the deltas of the
Sahamaloto and Anony rivers is to the west of Lake
Alaotra and has 8,880 hectares under cultivation. Another 3,000 hectares were to have been reclaimed by
the end of 1960. The Anony River area has an irrigation system built by the Sihanaka that, although useful,
functions with a great degree of irregularity. Improvement works have already started in the area. The
Sahamaloto River area is getting most of the attention,
however. Dikes are being built for approximately 9
miles along the river to control its meandering waters
and seasonal floods. Irrigation, which, under normal
climatic conditions, is carried out by deviating the
flow of the Sahamaloto and Sahamamy rivers, will be
regularized by means of two reservoirs costing 7 million

and 30 million francs CFA respectively. The larger of the two, the so-called Ampanamporo Reservoir, is to be completed first. The total cost is estimated at 185 million francs CFA, of which 150 million have been pledged under a four-year plan, while the remaining sum will be put at the disposal of the users.

The section of the Andilamena Plain, located about 36 miles north of the Alaotra Basin, has only 1,000 hectares under active cultivation, with another 2,500 hectares to be reclaimed. About 1,500 hectares are used for cattle grazing (there are over 200,000 head of cattle in the area). Because of numerous rock sills, the reclamation works will require over 450,000 cubic meters of terracing. The irrigation of lands to be reclaimed and the 1,000 hectares under cultivation are to be attained through the containment of up to 8 million cubic meters of water reserves by the construction of three barrages, to be placed at the head of the Maromandia, Bemaitso, and Ambodivato valleys. Over 130 million francs CFA are to be spent, with 120 million appropriated on paper under a four-year plan.

Subsector 23, located southwest of the lake, is the relatively least developed. According to latest estimates, over 30,000 hectares are cultivable and only a little over one third are under active cultivation at the present time. The rest is to be reclaimed and modernized at the cost of 2 billion francs CFA. Two main canals and a large reservoir (180 million cubic meters) are to be constructed for irrigation purposes. The project is to be accomplished by stages, beginning with the reclamation of some 10,000 hectares in the northern part of the sector. The reason for this particular selection is that the 10,000 hectares can be irrigated without the construction of the main reservoir. The cost of this stage is put at 800 million francs CFA. Since 1957, terracing, dike-building, and canal-construction works have been carried out on the left bank of the Sahabe River.

The northern part of Lake Alaotra has over 4,000 hectares under coordinated cultivation, and another 4,000, broken up into small plots, on which various types of produce are grown. No lands are to be reclaimed and no works are scheduled to take place in this particular area.

Of the 43,000 hectares under active cultivation in the entire Alaotra region (including lands which do not belong within any particular subsector), 35,000 hectares produce rice; 1,200, cassava; 1,600, peanuts; 200, tobacco; and the remaining 5,000, a large variety of vegetables and fruits. Taking the period 1951–56 together, the average annual production amounted to 60,000 tons of rice (about 50 per cent leaving the region), 8,000 tons of cassava (mostly tapioca), 2,000 tons of peanuts, and 100 tons of tobacco. There are over 3,000 ploughs in the area (two thirds belonging to Sihanaka farmers), 150 tractors (120 belonging to Europeans), a dozen steam shovels, three dozen bulldozers, between 20 and 30 threshers, over 100 trucks and railroad freight cars, and several freight craft on the lake itself. In addition to the railroad, there are over 400 miles of roads, eight post-office buildings, half a dozen minor airfields, and several mechanical workshops. There are two schools for European children; one integrated regional school; one professional secondary school with classes in arboriculture, applied agriculture, construction engineering, and applied mechanics for both Malagasy and Europeans; and sixty-nine makeshift classrooms for children under seven years of age. These are being replaced by relatively inexpensive one-classroom buildings designed to provide in the shortest possible time instruction for all children between the ages of six and fourteen. There is one large hospital and maternity ward, staffed mainly by European doctors; nine ambulance posts operated mostly by Malagasy doctors and nurses; and several mobile health-service and sanitation units. The concentrated development efforts undertaken after the revolt reflect what may be called an "area approach." It is no longer the practice to deal with different groups in different ways, but rather to treat the population of the area as a whole. While those already better off economically stand to gain the most from further development, the average Sihanaka farmer, sharecropper, and worker have at last been given the attention almost totally lacking in the past.

In terms of national production and consumption, the role of the Lake Alaotra region is, with minor differences, analogous to that of the other six development zones. Taken individually, each region is of only limited importance within the over-all context of the Malagasy economy. The Alaotra region meets its own alimentary needs with a measure of success. It is also able to export produce surpluses, which vary from one year to another. Owing to the presence of a considerable number of commercially minded Europeans, most of the yearly surpluses find their way into foreign markets, including the dollar zone, while on the whole the Malagasy benefit less than they should. It could be argued that export earnings may be reinvested either in the Alaotra region or elsewhere on the island and that the Malagasy economy would thus derive increasing benefits. Unfortunately, this is not the case. According to Maurice Aubry, the former President of the Tamatave Chamber of Commerce, Industry and Agriculture, the export earnings are very seldom reinvested either by individuals or by commercial enterprises operating in the province of Tamatave (the Lake Alaotra region being a part of this administrative province).

The production potential of Alaotra is considerable, perhaps greater than that of any of the other development zones. According to George Cours, who has directed its modern and progressive agricultural station during the last thirty years, the Alaotra region will, within the next five years, be able to produce over 200,000 tons of rice a year, 30,000 tons of cassava derivatives, and over 6,000 tons of peanuts. This does not seem to be an overestimate of the region's capacity, but its accuracy depends upon the completion of irrigation, reclamation, flood-control, and other construction projects that will, at the very least, cost some 2.5 billion francs CFA—a sum that can only come from France. Considering the immense economic problems facing France at present (the cost of the Algerian war being the major, but not the only, problem), it is unlikely that all of the needed money will be appropriated. This could retard the contemplated increase in the productive capacity of the Alaotra region by another five years. Essentially, the other six regions require the same commodity— money and more money.

Several further observations should be made about the economic picture in Madagascar at this juncture. The scope and the structure of the ten-year plan itself reveal eloquently the degree of underdevelopment in Madagascar.[8] Apart from the seven areas designated for development on an accelerated scale, only the social services have been extended throughout the island. Air transport has increased substantially in recent years, and some road improvements and port construction may also be noted. But internal communications remain insufficient, and neither *cabotage* nor air transport can be considered adequate for the development of a truly national economy at the present time.

In 1924, Malagasy farmers cultivated a total of 1.11 million hectares of land. In 1957, they were farming a total of 1.32 million hectares, most of it in small holdings. An increase of 200,000 hectares of cultivated land over a period of three decades may seem negligible in absolute terms. But it should be noted that to put one new acre under active cultivation involves expensive reclamation, flood-control, and other works given little attention prior to the 1950's. Besides, the average Malagasy family worked about 2 hectares of land in 1957, as contrasted to 4–5 hectares cultivated in 1924. Agricultural improvements and expansion are thus falling behind the population increase. It seems paradoxical that, on the one hand, depopulation prevents fuller agricultural and industrial development of the island, while, on the other hand, there does not seem to be enough land to go around. Yet the problem cannot be posed in terms of the mere existence of cultivable lands. Twenty-five years ago, Perrier de la Bathie estimated on the basis of an extensive vegetation study that about 8 million hectares of land exist in Madagascar that could be cultivated quite intensively without a rapid loss of soil fertility.[9] The figure has not as yet been challenged and may be accepted as reasonably accurate. Combining the Malagasy- and European-owned lands under actual cultivation (the latter are estimated at 1–2 million hectares), slightly less than one half of the total arable land is actively in use. The problem is essentially one of activating cultivable lands and then placing them under intensive cultivation. However, the cost of making these additional lands productive is staggering.

Underdevelopment also manifests itself in income figures. The average per-capita income in Madagascar (excluding salaried professions and workers) is about 20,000 francs, or $40. Nonagricultural workers get approximately four times as much, but, compared to those of local Europeans, their earnings are extremely low. In 1955, for example, 9,400 European employees earned some 4 billion francs, or $840 per capita, as against 11 billion francs earned by 137,000 Malagasy workers, or $160 per capita. Moreover, Creoles employed in the munitions arsenal in Diego-Suarez and Yemenite stevedores in the port of Majunga were among the best-paid "Malagasy" workers.

The administration of the ten-year plan, numerous and often overlapping soil and regional studies, the existence of six provinces involving at least forty-five different institutional budgets, as well as the other public-welfare activities during the last decade, have considerably extended the scope of the national bureaucracy. Excluding the police force, the army, the technical services, and units of local government, there are close to 18,000 administrative employees in Madagascar today. Between 50 and 60 per cent of the total annual budgets before 1959 covered administrative expenditures in the form of salaries and miscellaneous expenses. Considering the degree of development in Madagascar, the financial burden of an extended administrative machinery is indeed great. Prior to 1959, the constant deficits in the annual budgets had to be met through the FIDES, and as a result, funds earmarked for valid economic schemes had to be cut. Moreover, pressures for an increase in salaries and wage scales continued to mount, partly as a result of temporary inflation and partly because of a growing and more effective trade-union movement.[10]

The cost of government has been an important political issue and a strong argument for those who advocate the doctrine of centralism. It should be said, however, that several important developments in 1959 and 1960 force a reconsideration of the matter on purely economic and social grounds. In the first place, the economic effort begun at the turn of the 1950's is now beginning to pay off. For the first time, national budgets—those for 1959 and 1960—were balanced. The rising standard of living and the breakdown in strong regional autarchy have maximized the economic value of the considerable sums of money spent by salaried personnel. Since the creation of the Malagasy Republic in 1958, the administrative apparatus has been streamlined. Technical and scientific personnel outlays have been increased at the expense of clerical expenditures, and several salary categories have been scaled downward. The still-burdensome cost of administration must be considered from another point of view. Given the vastness and continental nature of Madagascar, there is little ground for assuming that centralization would greatly reduce the size of the administrative apparatus. Nor should the social implications of a relatively large bureaucracy be overlooked. As in most of Africa, "status" and government service go hand in hand, and a certain amount of featherbedding in local and provincial government may, in the long run, be cheaper for the island as a whole than would centralization.

The balance of trade has shifted significantly. During the 1936–46 period, Madagascar exported about 1.6 billion metric tons having a value of almost 9 billion francs, as against 1.1 million metric tons of imports valued at almost 7 billion francs. During a comparable period (1947 to 1957), about 2 million metric tons valued at 136.8 billion francs were exported, as against 3.6 million metric tons of imports having a value of 203.2 billion francs. In other words, after a trade surplus (in terms of value) of about 2 billion francs during the 1936–46 period, Madagascar developed a trade deficit of more than 66 billion francs during the ensuing decade. Even allowing for the steady inflation of the franc, the change is still significant.

Whatever the nature and scope of Madagascar's economic difficulties, and whatever degree of success may be expected in coping with them, two main facts stand out. The first is that Madagascar needs outside economic assistance. The second is that France has made a major effort during the last decade to maintain strong Franco-Malagasy bonds by means of far-reaching social and economic assistance—not, as some are apt to insist, by means of political and legal casuistry.

8

The Politics of Independence

The arbitrary division of the 1950's in earlier sections of this book should not lead the reader to the false assumption that Malagasy political aspirations died with the end of the 1947 revolt and were not reborn until June 23, 1956—the date of the *loi cadre*. The absence of overt expressions of local nationalism during the apparent lull of 1948–56 hides some of the important developments that took place beneath the façade of calm. These developments may be characterized as issues and groups, which became platforms and parties after 1956.

The first three postrevolt years left the hands of an overwhelmingly colonial-minded administration once again completely untied. While the National Assembly and the French Overseas Ministry in Paris were split into two groups having contradictory ideas on what attitude was to be adopted in Madagascar, the local administration continued to follow a "tough" line in the conduct of Malagasy affairs. As a result of this interlude of indecision in Paris, strict police surveillance of political "transgressors" in Madagascar continued, followed by arrests and forced-labor sentences. The only Malagasy left relatively unmolested were the adherents of the former PADESM, which had been outlawed along with the rest of the parties by martial law. Thus, under the guise of safeguarding "internal security," the local colonial administration was able during that period to prevent genuine nationalists from organizing and hence from making their legitimate grievances heard in Paris. It was during this time that the Communists made their debut in Madagascar.

The first important contact between Malagasy nationalists and the French Communist Party can be traced to 1945. According to a recorded statement made by Joseph Ravoahangy and quoted by Jacques Rabemananjara,

> If we wish to achieve something, we must do as the Vietnamese. I have not wasted my time in Paris, and some good work has been done. I have made contact with the Communist Party, and Raseta, Rakoto Ratsi-mamanga, and Raymond Rabemananjara are continuing the work on the spot and are in liaison with the influential people of that Party.[1]

This statement has often been quoted by French Rightists as "proof" that the 1947 revolt was Communist inspired, although that was by no means the case. It took approximately three to four years for a Communist cadre to form in Madagascar after 1947. After World War II, a number of Malagasy students (most of them Merina) went to Paris to work for graduate degrees. By 1948, there were about 200 Malagasy students there. The French Communist Party was the only one to make a concentrated, and hence successful, bid for their allegiance. In this, the Party had considerable help from Dr. Raseta and, to some extent,

Raymond Rabemananjara, a man much respected and admired by the students as one of the leading Malagasy intellectuals.

In 1950, many of the students returned to the island, having become both graduates of French universities and members of the Communist Party. Through social and cultural clubs and the trade-union movement, using the combined techniques of the *Sakelika* (cell), they helped form a skeleton organization that was later to become known as the Parti de l'Union du Peuple Malgache (PUPM). With the local nationalist movement badly disorganized after the revolt, the Communists and fellow travelers seized the opportunity to become the principal spokesmen for all shades of Malagasy nationalism. In 1950, a Solidarity Committee was formed in Tananarive, and, although it took no significant action until three years later, it helped keep alive the issue of independence and formulate the new cause of amnesty for all those who had been sentenced for their roles in the revolt. In addition, Communist infiltration of the trade-union movement led to forty minor strikes between 1951–53.

Besides the emergence of Communists in Madagascar, another important political development was the growing concern of the churches, and of a small but vocal group of liberal-minded Frenchmen led by former deputy Roger Duveau,* over the continuation of martial law, which effectively denied expression to Malagasy nationalist aspirations. To a large extent, the concern of the churches can be attributed to an enlightened

* Roger Duveau was greatly respected by the Malagasy. In 1953, he became Secretary of State for Overseas Territories and fought for the first amnesty laws. In 1956, he was elected by the Malagasy themselves as a deputy from the East Coast.

self-interest. The local Catholic and Protestant clergy was aware that their opposition to the 1947 uprising had identified them too closely with the colonial-minded administration, almost by default. Being convinced that, sooner or later, Madagascar would be governed by the Malagasy themselves, they sought ways to remove the stigma of association. A no less important consideration was the Christian ethic, which could remain indifferent neither to a continuing denial of civil and political liberties nor to the inroads of Communism in the island. When the Solidarity Committee issued an appeal for amnesty in 1953,[2] the Catholic newspaper *Lumière* expressed its agreement with the basically just demand of amnesty for all political prisoners, but refused to endorse the appeal because the Committee was a Communist front. In addition to lifting its voice in defense of Malagasy rights, the Catholic Church gave its vigorous support to two emerging nationalist parties of strong Christian Socialist tendency. One was the Parti Social Démocratique de Madagascar, led by Philibert Tsiranana, which had its main strength on the west coast; the other, the Union des Independents, was led by Stanislas Rakotonirina, who was to become Mayor of Tananarive in 1957.[3] Tsiranana was to become the first President of the Malagasy Republic in 1958. The Protestant Church, in turn, gave its support to a socialist group whose headquarters was in the port of Tamatave.

During this initial formation of parties, little rivalry could be observed between the two churches, although an insignificant number of Protestant clergy refused to condemn the Communist–extreme-nationalist alliance. The churches joined hands in a 1957 appeal to

the "people and the government of France"—the Ignace
Ramarosandratana appeal—which sought release for all
political prisoners in France and Madagascar.[4] In the
1957 municipal elections, some Protestants supported
Rakotonirina's mayoralty. Both churches helped form
an active anti-Communist trade-union movement—
which later split into two groups—and both were instrumental in securing the initial amnesty law of March
27, 1956. The law reduced the number of political
detainees from over 5,000 to about 1,400. To a lesser
extent, the churches also helped obtain additional amnesty legislation on March 18, 1958. The second amnesty
law granted a complete pardon to all the remaining
prisoners but, at the last minute, a rider was attached
to the bill whereby the "principal leaders of the former
MDRM" were to remain in exile in France until 1963.[5]
The rider affected some 200 individuals, as well as
Raseta, Ravoahangy, and Rabemananjara.

At the time of its introduction in 1956, the *loi cadre*
was simply an issue "within" the issues of independence
and amnesty.[6] Nationalist pressures and expectations
were already far more intense than overt political activity could suggest. As in most of the AOF and AEF, the
loi cadre was short-lived. The abolition of the dual
electoral college, the extension of suffrage, and the
granting of a more important role to African and
Malagasy ministers came at a time when nationalist
elites would accept nothing less than complete internal
autonomy—not to be hampered even by the possible
ceremonial presence of French high commissioners. Although the *loi cadre* was one of those measures that
"yielded too little, too late," the reaction of the
Malagasy to it brought to surface some interesting and

long-submerged attitudes that helped crystallize at least
one issue perhaps even more important to the future
of Madagascar and Africa than the issue of sovereignty.
This issue, which centers around the question of what
form of government would be best, can be described
as centralism versus federalism.

The general elections of March, 1957, also brought
to the surface eighteen different parties, ranging from
"unions for the defense of provincial interests" to those
making an islandwide bid for support.[7] A mere listing
of the names, the multiplicity and the numerical
strength of the eighteen parties cannot, however, convey
the real meaning of local forces. One can examine the
1957 electoral lists and yet learn little or almost nothing
of value. By coincidence, the number of parties corres-
ponded roughly to the number of principal tribal units
in the island. But it would be fruitless indeed to deduce
that there exist any similarities to the Nigerian experience or still less to that of the Congo, where forty-odd
tribal "parties" emerged shortly after the Brussels Conference in January, 1960. It would be closer to reality
to explain the nature of the emerging body politic of
Madagascar from the vantage point of the traditional
division between the coastal regions and the central
plateau. But to do so would be to oversimplify the
picture and hence to misjudge grossly the growing
importance of issues and alliances that cut across the
old lines of demarcation. One method of tracing the
evolution of political forces in Madagascar since 1956 is
to measure the attitude of each party toward the *loi
cadre* within the broader issue of independence. By
itself, this method is unsatisfactory, because the eighteen
parties can eventually be reduced to three or four

aggregates that are partly prototype parties and partly groupings clustered around individual leaders possessing a certain degree of charism. Another method, therefore, of underlining the significant aspects is to juxtapose parties and leaders, stressing outlooks and predilections. A third method is the focusing of attention on provincial as opposed to centralist tendencies, and to pinpoint the advocates of unitary and federalist forms of government.

In 1957, two leaders loomed large at one end of the nationalist spectrum: Jacques Rabemananjara and Stanislas Rakotonirina. The first, still in exile but closely in touch with his supporters on the island, represented what has been called the "progressive" nationalist group under the local leadership of Alexis Bezaka. The progressives were not opposed to the *loi cadre*. They accepted it as a purely transitional measure, urging rapid steps toward "final and complete" independence. They expressed the desire to remain within the French Union, but, at the same time, they argued that this desire could be translated into reality only *after* "complete independence" had been attained. Tamatave was the principal center of the progressives, but their appeal was broader than the location of party headquarters might suggest. Virtually all progressives demanded a strong unitary government. Both the progressives and the followers of Rakotonirina held the same views regarding unitary government, the transitional nature of the *loi cadre* and the need for complete independence. Rakotonirina, however, was personally willing to have Madagascar remain in the French Union without making this contingent upon the previous attainment of independence (although in 1958, he did vote against Madagascar's membership in the Community). At that time, the main difference between the two progressive groups concerned relations with the Communist–extreme-nationalist alliance. The followers of Rakotonirina's Union des Indépendants (UI) were against any tactical "compromise" with this alliance, while the progressives broke into two factions: the left-wing Union des Intellectuels et Universitaires Malgaches (UNIUM), led by a Dr. Ramangasoavina; and the right-wing Union Nationale Malgache (UNAM), led by Alexis Bezaka. The UNIUM was not Communist-dominated, but much of its membership leaned heavily toward Marxist dogmas and did not consider cooperation with Communists a political problem. The UNAM continued the progressive opposition to both Communists and radical nationalists as well as to Catholic-inspired Christian Socialist parties. The views of Jacques Rabemananjara (befriended in France by François Mitterrand and Pierre Mendès-France) and Alexis Bezaka were an amalgam of secular and Christian socialism, wherein the canons of centralism were intertwined with notions of individual freedom. Prior to the formation of the Malagasy Republic, the progressives formed a flexible alliance known as the Parti Populaire Malgache (PPM).

Further to the left of the UI and the PPM was a party known at first as Rassemblement du Peuple Malgache (RPM) and later as Union des Démocrates Malgaches (UDM). The port of Diego-Suarez was the stronghold of this party, and shortly after its formation (1956–57) it seemed as if the UDM sought to inherit the mantle of the prerevolt MDRM. The UDM flatly rejected the provisions of the *loi cadre* and demanded immediate independence (*Fahaleovantena Tantarara*), pledging that Madagascar would not join the French Union. Still later, the party changed its name to Congrès de l'Indépendance de Madagascar, finally opting for a Malagasy equivalent, Ankoton'ny Kongresi'ny Fahaleovantenan Madagasikara (AKFM). Radical and isolationist in outlook, Communist in organization and in tactics, the AKFM developed two main branches: one in Diego-Suarez, led by Justin Bezara (ex-member of the MDRM); the other in Tananarive, led by a relatively moderate Merina Communist, the Rev. Richard Andriamanjato, who was to oust Rakotonirina as mayor of Tananarive in October, 1959. Reference has already been made to the PUPM. Renaming itself Union du Peuple Malgache, this party suddenly disappeared in a rather curious fashion. At the end of 1959, it merged completely with the AKFM. But several dozen of its militant members led by Mme. Giselle Rabesahala, (who claims to be the only Malagasy woman ever to have shaken hands with Stalin), almost overnight became the leading group within the AKFM. Andriamanjato was temporarily ousted from the high council of the AKFM, and the party assumed an even more radical attitude. This can be explained by two events, one in France and the other in Madagascar itself. The Catholic-inspired Christian Socialists controlled the government of the new Republic of Madagascar, and in France the French Communist Party had lost considerable power as a result of the De Gaulle victory. The De Gaulle-Tsiranana alliance led the Central Committee of the AKFM to conclude that only the most militant attitude could give it an opportunity to capture the reins of government before any major benefits to the Malagasy people could evolve out of Franco-Malagasy cooperation.

Contrary to claims made by some Western observers, the AKFM, ideologically, is not an orthodox Communist Party. It is an amalgam of Marxist-oriented nationalists whose ideal is a corporate, almost fascist, state; of Communists whose primary loyalty belongs to the French CP; and of the many leftist intellectuals on the island. Moreover, the AKFM membership includes a large Merina segment, much as did the PDM in 1946. The AKFM differs from the rest of the parties in two other respects. It does not lack funds, most of which seem to come from abroad—although this cannot be proved. It is extremely well organized, having a youth organization (AJDM), a trade union (FISEMA), an amnesty and solidarity committee (COSOMA), and a publishing house reportedly called the "Malagasy Friendship Association." The Communists have worked hard for several years to capture the intellectual element and to reorient the island toward the Soviet concept of neutrality widely disseminated at the Cairo Solidarity Conference—i.e., the type of neutrality whereby a country shows economic and cultural preference for the Communist bloc on domestic and foreign-policy issues alike. Malagasy delegates were sent to various "freedom congresses" in Budapest, Warsaw, and Prague even before the emergence of the AKFM. One of Justin Bezara's associates, Maurice Razhaofera, attended the Cairo Solidarity Conference as the "representative of Madagascar." [8] The main headquarters of the FISEMA is in Paris. The AJDM finances students abroad, either in Paris, where visiting Malagasy students are sponsored by the several-hundred-strong Association des Étudiants d'origine Malgache, or else in satellite capitals or

Moscow. According to a recent unofficial estimate, there are some 150 Malagasy students in Moscow alone. Through its affiliates the AKFM issues its own publications and has in the past supplied material to the Soviet Academy of Sciences. An example of this cooperation is a 107-page article on Madagascar by A. S. Orlova in a 1958 issue of *Afrikansky Etnograficbesky Sbornik* published by the Soviet Academy of Sciences. The article does not discuss current affairs or the Franco-Malagasy relations, but it reveals a high degree of general knowledge about the island.

Finally, at the other end of the nationalist spectrum there may be found two parties more or less comparable to the RDA. Both were completely opposed to the alliances of the Left, sought gradual independence, and considered French Union membership not only desirable but necessary. They were not initially in favor of a centralist form of government. These two parties were the Parti Social Démocratique Malgache (PSDM) and the Union Démocratique et Sociale de Madagascar (UDSM). Led by Philibert Tsiranana and ex-senator Norbert Zafimahova, respectively, the two organizations were supported by about twelve smaller associations in the provinces of Majunga, Tuléar, and Fianarantsoa. Most of the Malagasy governments since 1958 have been composed of members of these two parties.

By the end of 1958, the *loi cadre* was a forgotten issue. It would not be long before sovereignty and amnesty would likewise become issues of the past. What new issues would emerge and what would the parties look like in the new Republic of Madagascar?

To start with the economic difficulties facing the island, it is worth noting that the economic proposals of the genuine nationalists in their various policy statements were seldom detailed and specific and often of a very general nature. The Christian Socialists (PSDM-UDSM-UI) promised an agrarian reform consisting primarily of distribution of state-owned lands to Malagasy farmers, a balanced economy in which equal attention would be given to agriculture and industry, creation of an atmosphere of confidence conducive to foreign-capital investment, an attack on illiteracy, full employment for workers, tax relief and debt forgiveness, and an adequate income for the entire working population.[9] The Progressives (PPM-RDM-UNAM) promised to "create a real and sound democracy, as far removed from a capitalist democracy that would permit the continuation of social injustices as from a totalitarian democracy that would transform freedom into a special privilege for one party, one caste, and one class." [10] It further pledged to erect an entirely new economic structure, one that would encourage both public and private investments, and promised to implement an agrarian reform based on the distribution of untenanted land.

The vagueness, whether deliberate or not, of these economic programs is apparent. An agrarian reform based on the distribution of state-owned or untenanted land must take into consideration that the Malagasy farmers cannot afford the reclamation, flood control, and irrigation needed to bring each new acre under cultivation. A balanced economy in an overwhelmingly agricultural society must be preceded by a great deal of groundwork regarding the channeling of unproductive farm labor into other sectors of production, by greater knowledge of natural resources, a knowledge essential to increased investments of foreign private

capital and to the expansion of industrialization. Full
employment for workers and adequate income for the
entire population are future goals, not practical
measures. Common to all genuine nationalist groups is
the desire—practical or not—for the welfare state,
without a program for how a welfare state is to be
achieved. It is easy to criticize the shortcomings of proposals for the development of underdeveloped areas
like Madagascar, but in doing so, one must not lose
sight that the economic policy best suited to the growth
and development of a country is not based primarily
on economic issues, but on the assumptions concerning
the type of government most likely to bring about a
higher general standard of living.

The advocates of federal government wish to preserve
the present provincial structure. The richer and more
developed regions do not relish sharing the wealth
with the poorer ones, but those in favor of federalism
do not object to the primacy of national government
in Tananarive in matters of public investment, foreign
trade, and foreign economic relations. Those advocating
a unitary system have a simpler case, in that the abolition of provinces would vest all matters of economic
policy in the hands of a national government. One
of the strongest arguments for the preservation of the
provincial structure has been based on the coastal
regions' fear of central-plateau domination of the rest
of the island. Looked at in this way, federalism is
not so much a credo as a reaction to possible Merina
supremacy in modern dress. There are several forces,
on the other hand, that offset economic regionalism
and fear of Merina supremacy. In the first place,
provincial division is regarded by many as the legacy

of *panjakana*, or colonial rule. Secondly, it is extremely easy to make a case against the high cost of the provincial arrangement. Third, unitary government is seen not as a danger to democracy but, in fact, as its necessary precondition. The economic arguments and the conception of the democratizing role of unitary government have been instrumental in creating pressure for national unity, which means different things to different people but which acts as an antiprovincial agent. Finally, there is a real temptation to look upon the establishment of strong central government as a measure diminishing the possibility of dislodging the party in power, and it is hard to believe that there is any party in Madagascar that would reject the relative security of centralism once it gained power or once it were assured of gaining power in the near future.

At the beginning of 1959, the profederalist nationalists were in power (PSDM-UDSM, joined by Tamatave's leading representative, Alexis Bezaka), and the economic approach of the genuine nationalists, whether in the government or in the opposition, does not differ too greatly. The PSDM, UDSM (which has since changed its name to Union des Sociaux-Démocrates de Madagascar, or UDGM), PPM, RDM, UNAM, RCM (Rassemblement Chrétien de Madagascar, a new splinter group opposing the PSDM but not the government itself) and UI are all in agreement regarding the need for further large-scale assistance from France. In their different ways, all veer toward the idea of the welfare state. The main difference is that the first two parties play a major role in the government of Madagascar, while the others represent an opposition that varies in intensity at given times but that, on the whole, has not been remiss in observing the "rules of the game." The Malagasy themselves tend to describe the five more or less moderate parties as a nonabsolute and fluctuating opposition. The word "fluctuating" is particularly useful in describing the nature of the opposition during the first quarter of 1959. While sharing a measure of unity in being against the government, the moderate opposition apparently could not decide how to proceed. It must have felt that little was to be gained by increasing the pressure for independence and amnesty, both of which were regarded not only as integral parts of the general policy of the Tsiranana Government, but also as *faits accomplis* vis-à-vis France. Thus the electorate's approval of the new Constitution by a vote of 1,368,059 to 392,557 also reflected Malagasy confidence that independence and amnesty would be granted without undue delay.

Economic issues were not sufficiently clear-cut to provide a basis for a new political strategy. The Christian Socialists, who, prior to 1958, had been the foremost champions of federalism, were now in power and called for national unity, which had been a motto and a political weapon of both the Progressives and Independents at the time when independence and amnesty were the foremost issues in the island. Relations between the government and its moderate opposition consequently assumed the character of intramural fights having little bearing on substantive issues but, rather, mirroring the conflicts among personalities in and out of power. Tsiranana was thus accused of being too subservient to French interests. In turn, he condemned those who had cast their votes against the French Community. Stanislas Rakotonirina in particular was singled out for attack because he had voted "no" in the referendum of September 28, 1958, after implying that he would support it. As a result of the Tsiranana-Rakotonirina disagreement, a number of adherents rallied behind the AKFM.

Partly because of the new and unexpected support and partly because of the growing international prestige of former French Guinea, the AKFM sought once more to rally all opposition parties and groups in the island, or more specifically in the towns. After a convention held in August, 1959, the AKFM revived the issues of amnesty and independence with new vigor. In October of that year, it won the municipal elections in Tananarive, recaptured the mayoralty of Diego-Suarez, and made a good showing in Tamatave. After the change of leadership in the last days of 1959, the AKFM advanced a newly revised economic platform calling for the nationalization of all private enterprise, the removal of all non-Malagasy from local and national government posts, and the introduction of a new currency designed to remove Madagascar from the franc zone. The AKFM position on the question of Franco-Malagasy relations remained ambiguous, however. Despite its disagreement with the AKFM, the moderate opposition found itself forced to side with some of the party's demands. In response to the pressures of the opposition, the Malagasy National Assembly voted in favor of an amnesty law. Conscious of Sékou Touré's increasing—if only temporary—popularity in the United States, Tsiranana, accompanied by Félix Houphouet-Boigny of the Ivory Coast, journeyed to New York and Washington in November, 1959. Upon his return to Madagascar in December, 1959, Tsiranana announced to the National

Assembly that he had asked President de Gaulle for talks on the issue of independence of Madagascar. In January, 1960, Tsiranana asked the National Assembly for special powers for a one-year period in order to implement the transfer of sovereignty from France to Madagascar. These powers were granted. In February, 1960, Jacques Rabemananjara and Joseph Ravoahangy indicated support for the Tsiranana policies. Also in February, 1960, negotiations between Madagascar and France began in Paris. On April 2, 1960, agreements on the independence of Madagascar were signed in Paris by Tsiranana and French Premier Debré. On June 26, 1960, the independence of the Malagasy Republic was proclaimed in Tananarive.[11]

In 1960, the Tsiranana Government made efforts to secure support on a national scale. Between January 19 and 25, Tsiranana visited eleven cities in an effort to offset the opposition. In February, 1960, he sent two assistants to carry on the campaign under the slogan of "Cooperation and work—not anarchy and xenophobia." In March, 1960, the *Journal Officiel de Madagascar* published the text of two ordinances making it illegal to send telegrams "judged contrary to the public order" and to distribute aid (after the highly destructive floods of 1959) without "prior government clearance." The first decree clearly was aimed at preventing the duplication of the famous March 27, 1947, telegram; while the second sought to block the Communist and crypto-Communist elements in the island from exploiting the relatively meager flood-relief funds supplied by the satellite countries for propaganda purposes.

On the whole, however, the present government has so far shown no inclination to curtail civil liberties, and the opposition (both moderate and extremist) enjoys undisputed freedom. Although the government controls the radio station and some newspapers (*Vao-Vao*, for example) freedom of the press continues to be very real. The provincial structure remains intact, but Malagasy are steadily replacing foreigners at all administrative levels. Recently, Malagasy deputies voted a reduction of their own salaries in an effort to curtail administrative costs throughout the island.

In the economic field, the Tsiranana Government also moved quickly in late 1959 and 1960. Rejecting all dogmatic approaches to economic problems, Tsiranana turned to the agricultural sector as the economic sector most in need of funds and effort. Madagascar also joined the European Economic Community. The African Economic Cooperation Commission held an international conference in Madagascar in February, 1960. Efforts to attract private industry were increased. Alfred Ramangasoavina, the Minister for Industry, and Victor Miadana, Secretary of State for Economic Affairs, visited the United States in search of capital investments. Representatives of several U.S. firms (notably Westinghouse and Koppers) also visited Madagascar, and a leading American network sought affiliated television rights. The *fonds d'aide et cooperation* credits for 1960 were likely to be in the neighborhood of $25 million, while the EEC pledge for 1960 amounted to about $14 million, most of it earmarked for improvements in communications and agriculture.

The economic, social, and political drive of the Tsiranana Government leaves the extreme opposition in the island with less and less support. Like former Premier Adnan Menderes in Turkey, Tsiranana has based his power on the support of the rural population, i.e., the vast majority. Unlike Menderes', however, his economic policies are sound, and he has permitted the opposition to challenge the government within the established limits. Because the pro-Communist AKFM holds considerable power in two of the five major cities of the island, it is still a dangerous opponent, but an alliance of the Christian Socialists, led by Tsiranana, with the Progressives, led by Jacques Rabemananjara, would serve to put the AKFM out of serious competition. Two additional safeguards are needed to insure the future of Madagascar against extremism and isolationism. One is foreign aid and private investment. With adequate means at its disposal, any government in a little-developed area can show immediate and tangible results, for just everything is in need of improvement—from village schools to dams to coal mines. It does matter a great deal, however, what *kind* of government begins to show results first, for more often than not, the first government to rule a newly independent country leaves an indelible stamp on its social and political life. The second safeguard may be copied from the Lebanese experience, at least in spirit. The Malagasy Constitution could contain a built-in provision specifying that, for a given span of time, the President must come from a group other than the Merina to accelerate the breaking down of old barriers. The same provision could make it mandatory for the President of the National Assembly to be a Merina.[12]

CONCLUSION

Africa—vast, difficult, and diverse—continues to elude not only the pamphleteer who writes with self-righteous indignation and a disregard for facts, but also the scholar who tries to write with knowledge and sympathy. At times, Africa is written and talked about as if it did not exist at all or as if it were an exclusive game preserve for reputable specialists. For some pundits, Africa holds no secrets. For others, Africa is so "complex" that nothing must be said about it. There are visionaries who believe that the only contribution still to be made in Africa is the building of dams and bridges. There are scholars who tend to regard all others interested in Africa as parvenus and opportunists, crowding what until recently was a restricted field. The parrotlike repetition of African views as the beginning and end of all knowledge, or the almost pathological reactions to African events or statements, reveal more about our own predilections than about Africa.

Some are willing to spend the next decade in silence, digging Africa's history out of the ruins, oral traditions, artifacts, old manuscripts, archives, art, bones, crop plants, climatic patterns, stereotypes, and gross misconceptions. Others cannot find either the modesty or the time to remain quiet, fearing that Africa will not wait for the findings. The policy-maker who sees in the encouragement of separatism the path to anti-Communist bastions rubs shoulders with a more sophisticated colleague who not only holds that empathy will make Africans out of us all, but also that there would be no conflict of priorities if Africa could only be understood. The colonial-minded keep spinning the web of their mythology around political conservatives, while the liberal insists that the phenomenon of anticolonial mythology simply does not exist.

The elusiveness of Africa has imposed what appear to be only two alternatives: not to generalize at all or to do so almost exclusively from assumptions based in part on the necessarily sketchy familiarity with the continent as a whole and in part on the intellectual crosscurrents that reflect the moral and political climate of our times. Perhaps the second alternative is the most difficult to escape from and—for the serious student— to live with. Without any claims to immunity, it seems appropriate to conclude this brief volume with one or two observations of a general nature.

One of the most visible and most powerful trends in Africa today is a managerial revolution—central to which is the notion of efficiency—under the sole guardianship of planners and managers who are the products of modern education. In the words of Jacques Rabemananjara:

> Do not search in Dakar, do not search in Brazzaville for the intense, ardent presence of Africa. It dwindles, it suffocates with every new day. It freezes from a cold close to agony. Day and night, the foremost task to which the

efforts of men are addressed is to erase its traces everywhere, to dim its luster—as if there were an addiction to ritual impelled by a devotion to the cult of modern gods.

It is out of this cult of modernism rather than any discernible ideology rooted in the African past or entering present-day Africa from other regions that the political cart is placed in front of the economic horse. The notion of national unity, whereby the party and the people become interchangeable, is seen as an integral part of progress; the strong central government as the *sine qua non* of economic development. Tribes, groups, factions, and, ultimately, individuals are under growing pressure to observe the maxims of self-sacrifice, self-discipline, and duty to the motherland. No nation —be it new or old, rich or poor, advanced or retarded— can escape the need for and the curse of its bureaucracy.

The same centripetal forces that operate in Africa are certainly to be found in Madagascar. But at least one major feature of the island should force the African or the Western efficiency expert to reassess the gospel that grassroot dynamism in "underdeveloped" areas must be fostered from the top.

The absence of a political monolith in recent Malagasy history has in no way hampered either economic development, which compares favorably with that of Guinea or Ghana, or the orderly functioning of political, social, and economic institutions. The remarkable degree of tolerance within Malagasy society is not simply the end product of an outlook shared by most of the population. It is even more than "pluralism," which grasps the obvious advantages of compromise and live-and-let-live. This tolerance is also a product of rather complex and interlocking relationships that have been *allowed* to develop and are *not* being sacrificed to the canons of centralism.[1] Local government in Madagascar is no mere training grounds for selected young men or an extension of Tananarive bureaucracy. Through rural, municipal, and provincial councils, as well as through elected provincial assemblies, local government plays an extremely important and real role. The entire system of interrelated units is buttressed further by the numerous independent cooperative associations—such as the *Fokon'olona* in the villages—and unions, trade associations, and chambers of commerce in the townships.

The administrative governmental divisions in Madagascar do not coincide with the tribal lines, as they do in the former Belgian Congo. The economic effort during the past decade, particularly in the zones of Mahavavy-Sambirano, Basse-Betsiboka, Morondava, Alaotra, Pangalanes, Mandrare, and Mangoky-Sakoa does not fit into any tribal patterns. Educational expenditures and efforts, in which both the federal government and its provincial counterparts participate, are made in inverse proportion to the degree of literacy in each province as a matter of deliberate policy aimed at wiping out the disparities. In 1959, the highest percentage of literacy—74 per cent—existed in Tananarive Province and the lowest—22 per cent—in that of Tuléar. The national average, however, has now reached 50 per cent.

Tribalism cannot be eliminated by fiat, but only by slow and gradual social change, and this, too, is a matter of deliberate policy that does show results. To give an example: A Tsimihety farmer in the province of

Majunga and his opposite number in the province of Diego-Suarez tend to associate their immediate interests with the communal cooperative and market association to which each belongs. Hence, they indirectly take part in two separate provincial structures with often conflicting interests. Furthermore, both men participate in this process not so much as Tsimihety but as agricultural workers. It is only on general issues that both are likely to be affected by their tribal affiliation. As a tribe, for example, the Tsimihety are solidly behind their native son Philibert Tsiranana and tend to support his policies. During the 1958 referendum, 93 per cent of the voters in the province of Majunga cast a "yes" ballot. The rural Tsimihety vote in Diego-Suarez Province prevented, by a two-to-one margin, a victory for those opposing the referendum provisions.

While Madagascar's highly decentralized system should not be confused with federalism, it does resemble a federalist arrangement, in that the central government becomes an arbiter as well as partner, a kind of middle link that lengthens the chain. Given the lack of an indigenous oligarchy—for the Merina no longer occupy a position similar to that of the Ethiopian Amhara—it is not difficult to see that the mechanics of solidarity require the national arena, while regional diversity provides sufficient tensions for a social and economic dynamism not imposed from the top. The road to political unity and economic growth, helped considerably by internal migrations, has not led through the gate of centralism.

If, as some have observed, present-day Guinea is to Africa what Cuba is to Latin America (a rather strained analogy), then in an even more real sense Madagascar

can be compared to an African Puerto Rico on the
eve of its Operation Bootstrap. The West should not
lose sight of the beneficial influence the Malagasy have
come to exert on the French-speaking states of West
and Equatorial Africa since 1958. Africa itself could
do no worse than to study the Malagasy experience, for
nowhere is there another miniature continent with
which it has as much in common. The social sciences,
too, have much to learn from Madagascar—certainly
much more than how rice is grown or how someone's
"pet" tribe lives. If one wishes to examine such subjects as social fragmentation or homogeneity; the relationship between dialects and an indigenous lingua
franca; autarchy or economic symbiosis; white settler
failures and indigenous successes; color bars and mixed
marriages; the interaction of ancestor worship and
Islam or Christianity; unproductive labor and highly
efficient communal enterprise; the role of predestination in a tribal economy; pastoral and sedentary outlooks; indigenous and Western concepts or social stratification; various types of chief, council, or shaman rule;
the many shades of colonial policy and administration
tested for the first time in Madagascar, to say nothing
of an unusually rich history—all will be found in the
island. While not a "crisis" area by current standards
of measurement, Madagascar is today a battleground for
forces toward which none can be neutral. If this lesson
is not lost upon the student of Africa who reads this
volume, its purpose will be more than attained.

Notes

Chapter 1
Notes, Problems, and Sources

1. Guillaume Grandidier, "La France et Madagascar: 1527–1805," *Madagascar* (Paris: Cahiers Charles de Foucauld, 1950), p. 51.
2. To what extent Islamic influences have been felt in Madagascar is a matter of some controversy. In the past, scholars interested in the island have amassed an impressive amount of data that tend to support the view of a very high degree of Islamic influence. Gabriel Ferrand's *Les Musulmans à Madagascar et aux Iles Comores,* 2 vols. (Paris, 1891–93 and 1902), though outdated, remains one of the finest works on the subject. His two monographs, "Les Migrations Musulmanes et Juives à Madagascar," *Revue de l'Histoire des Religions (Annales du Musée Guimet),* III, 381–417, and "Tribus Musulmanes du Sud-Est de Madagascar," *Revue de Madagascar* (Paris, 1903), are also worth reading. (The offices of the *Revue de Madagascar* were transferred from Paris to Tananarive in 1933.) For a somewhat different point of view, namely that Islamic influences may be traced to Indonesia rather than Africa, see the first volume of Alfred and Guillaume Grandidier's *Ouvrages Anciens Concernant Madagascar* (Paris, 1903). More recent views on Islam and its relative impact among the Malagasy hold that the degree of Islamic influence has been exaggerated. For the more recent views, see, for example: "L'Islam en Afrique Noire Française," *La Documentation Fran-*

çaise, *Notes et Études Documentaires* (hereafter referred to as NED), No. 1152 (June 26, 1949); R. P. Venait's article in *En Terre d'Islam* (Paris), 3d series, No. 39 (3d quarter, 1947); Col. Trouchet, *Initiations à la Connaissance de l'Islam* (Paris, 1949), particularly the map in the appendix; and Dominique Sourdel, *L'Islam* (Paris, 1949). For a view that seeks to balance divergent arguments, see the brief but informative article by Charles Poirier, "Influences Islamiques de Madagascar," *Madagascar* (Paris, 1950), pp. 272–83. Regardless of the differences, Islamic traditions and customs are still found among 400,000 or more Malagasy and tend to be felt more along the coast than in the interior of the country.

3. George Peter Murdock, *Africa: Its People and Their Cultural History* (New York: McGraw-Hill Book Co., 1959), p. 212.

4. "Tache Pigmentaire Héréditaire et Origines des Malgaches," *Revue Anthropologique* (Paris), January–March, 1940, pp. 5–128.

5. Murdock, *op. cit.*, pp. 212–21.

6. Several sources give a good physical description of the island. For an excellent guide to the sources, see Elisabeth Platt, "Madagascar: Great Isle, Red Isle," *Geographical Review*, XXVII (1937), 301–08.

7. C. Heine, *Madagaskar* (Hamburg, 1932), figure 9.

8. For a chart of average monthly rainfall in fourteen different places in Madagascar, see *La France de l'Océan Indien* (Paris, 1952), VIII, 20. For concise accounts of the climate in the isle, see Dudley L. Stamp, *Africa: A Study in Tropical Development* (3d ed.; New York: John Wiley & Sons, 1957), p. 509; and Charles Poisson, "Les Climats de Madagascar," *Comptes Rendus du Congrès International de Géographie* (Paris), III, No. 1 (1933), 333–39.

9. W. A. Hance, "Transportation in Madagascar," *Geographical Review*, XLVIII (1958), 45–68.

10. Alfred and Guillaume Grandidiers' monumental *Ethnographie de Madagascar* (5 vols. in 4—2,251 pp.) was

published in Paris in 1908, 1914, 1917, and 1928, respectively. No comparable work has been written since. Moreover, vols. 2 and 3, which are primarily concerned with the family, clan, and tribe are over forty years old. Other single works, like J. Aubrey's *La Tribu des Sakalava* (Paris, 1910), and Hughes Berthier's *Rapport sur les Races de Madagascar* (Paris, 1911), are also dated. Berthier's later work, *Notes et Impressions sur les Moeurs et Coutumes du Peuple Malgache,* was published in Tananarive in 1933. Periodicals like the *Revue de Madagascar* (1933–39, and the new series published since 1949), *Memoires de L'Académie Malgache* (1926–49) and the current *Bulletin de Madagascar* offer occasional articles, many of them quite good, but none sufficiently extensive for a study in depth. The *Notes, Reconnaissances et Explorations* (5 vols., 1897–1901), and the *Antananarivo Annual* combine the disadvantages of being dated with the virtue of brevity.

11. Among the works published during the last decade, the following are noteworthy: Raymond W. Rabemananjara, *Madagascar, Histoire de la Nation Malgache* (Paris, 1952), and *Madagascar sous la Rénovation Malgache* (Paris, 1953); Dama Ntsoha (pseud.), *Histoire Politique et Religieuse des Malgaches* (Tananarive, 1955); Richard Andriamanjato, *Tsiny et le Tody dans la Pensée Malgache* (Paris, 1957). French contributions of note include: Raymond Decary, *Moeurs et Coutumes des Malgaches* (Paris, 1951); Louis Molet, *Le Bain Royal à Madagascar* (Tananarive, 1956); O. Mannoni, *Psychologie de la Colonisation* (Paris, 1950); Louis Chevalier, *Madagascar, Populations et Ressources* (Paris, 1952); Hildebert Isnard, *Madagascar* (Paris, 1955); G. Condaminas, *Fokon'olona et Communautés Rurales en Imerina* (Paris, 1960); and Hubert Deschamps, *Histoire de Madagascar* (Paris, 1960). The last is the most compressed work, covering virtually every sphere of endeavor. Most of the above-cited volumes treat the major changes in Malagasy society in a gen-

eral way. Together with an earlier, pioneering work by R. Decary and R. Castel, *Modalités et Conséquences des Migrations Intérieures Recentes des Populations Malgaches* (Tananarive, 1941), based on the 1936 census, Chevalier's study and Hubert Deschamps' 1959 work on internal migrations (see note 15 below) offer invaluable information.

12. A. Dandouau and G.-S. Chapus (eds.), *Histoire des Populations de Madagascar* (Paris, 1952), pp. 28, 35.
13. "Esquisse de la Mentalité Malgache," *Revue Psychologique des Peuples*, XIV, No. 1 (1959), 25–40.
14. For the most concise discussion of the various possibilities regarding immigration to Madagascar, see Chevalier, *op. cit.*, pp. 191–99.
15. Deschamps, *Les Migrations Intérieures Passées et Presentes à Madagascar* (Paris, 1959), pp. 266, 268, 276.
16. Hance, *op. cit.*, p. 56.
17. See Deschamps, "Conceptions, Problèmes et Sources de l'Histoire de Madagascar," *The Journal of African History*, I, No. 2, 249–56.

Chapter 2
THE MALAGASY: PORTRAIT OF A PEOPLE

1. "Notes on the Antanakarana," *Antananarivo Annual,* No. 3 (1877), p. 28.
2. Dandouau and Chapus, *op. cit.*, p. 28.
3. Charles Robequain, *Madagascar et les Bases Dispersées de l'Union Française* (Paris, 1958), p. 201.
4. Probably due to the remnants of Islamic tradition, which, with the exception of the Comoro Islands, is strongest among some of the Sakalava and Antemoro clans. (See Jean Manicacci, *L'Archipel des Comores* [Tananarive, 1939]; U. Faurec, *L'Archipel aux Sultans Batailleurs* [Tananarive, 1941]; also *Encyclopédie Coloniale et Maritime* [Paris, 1947], II.
5. Dandouau and Chapus, *op. cit.*, p. 31.
6. *Ibid.*, p. 89.
7. G. Saron and R. Lisan, *Madagascar et les Comores* (a

pictorial report) (Paris, 1953), photograph and caption 134 to *Tombeau Mahafaly.*

8. An interesting analogy of the possibilities can be found in E. A. Kinch, "Social Effects of the Oil Industry in Iraq," *Labor Review,* LXXV (March, 1957), 193–206.

9. Dandouau and Chapus, *op. cit.,* p. 72.

10. *Antananarivo Annual,* III (1887), 84–85.

11. J. Faublée, *La Cohésion des Sociétés Bara* (Paris, 1953), p. 5.

12. *Ibid.,* p. 87.

13. *Antananarivo Annual,* II (1876), 74.

14. Robequain, *op. cit.,* p. 139.

15. Dandouau and Chapus, *op. cit.,* p. 41.

16. P. Launois, *Madagascar Hier et Aujourd'hui* (Paris, 1947), p. 116.

17. Deschamps, *Les Migrations Intérieures à Madagascar* (Paris, 1959), p. 64.

18. R. L. Beals and Harry Hoijer, *An Introduction to Anthropology* (New York: The Macmillan Company, 1953), p. 395.

19. See Gustave Julien, "Pages Arabico-Madécasses," *Annals of the Academy of Colonial Science* (Paris, 1929), pp. 1–123; the *"Sora-Bé Manuscripts* (Paris, 1952), pp. 279–83, also manuscript facsimile opposite p. 263; and "The Influence of the Arabs on the Malagasy Language," *Antananarivo Annual,* II (1876), 75–91.

20. Quoted by Solomon Chase Osborn in *Madagascar: The Land of the Man-eating Tree* (New York, 1924)—the only work by an American to deal with Madagascar in general. The pirates had at one time proclaimed Madagascar the "Republic of Libertalia." The best work on the pirates is Deschamps' *Les Pirates à Madagascar aux XVIIᵉ et XVIIIᵉ Siècles* (Paris, 1949).

21. Osborn, *op. cit.,* p. 96.

22. Walter Hamond, *Madagascar* (London, 1640), Preface; see also *Antananarivo Annual,* II (1876), 51–56.

23. E. David-Bernard, *La Conquête de Madagascar* (Paris, 1943), p. 23.

24. Adolphe Bruniquel, "Les Malgaches à Travers l'Histoire," in *Madagascar* (Paris, 1950), p. 27.

25. James Sibree, "The Sakalava: Their Origin, Conquests and Subjection," *Antananarivo Annual,* IV (1878), 58.

26. See P. Cultru, *Un Empereur de Madagascar au XVIIIᵉ Siècle: Benyowsky* (Paris, 1906), and M. Lepecki, *M. A. Hrabia Beniowski, Zdobywca Madagaskaru* (Lvov, 1938). (This Polish-language work is perhaps the best ever published on Benyowsky.) Benyowsky's memoirs were published in 1791 in French.

27. No single field of study concerning Madagascar has received greater attention than the history of the Merina state, and it would be impossible to list more than a dozen of the best: Julien, *Institutions Politiques et Sociales de Madagascar,* 2 vols. (Paris, 1909); C. P. Borrel, *Le Code de 305 Articles* (Paris, 1931); Rev. Malzac, *Histoire du Royaume Hova Depuis Ses Origines Juisqu'a la Fin* (Tananarive, 1912). The author has made extensive use of a four-volume classic written in Malagasy by Rev. Callet under the title *Tantaran'ny Andriana eto Madagascar,* which is being translated into French. Unlike most works on the subject, it does not approach the Merina monarchy as an institution but rather in terms of individual rulers. J. Cahuzac, *Essai sur les Institutions et le Droit Malgaches* (Paris, 1902–14); P. Launois, *L'État Malgache et ses Transformations Avant le Régime Français* (Paris, 1923). *The Bulletin de l'Académie Malgache* is also a rich source of some of the finest literature on the subject.

28. See "La Rivalité Franco-Anglaise," in Launois, *op. cit.,* pp. 156–81, for the French version, and S. Passfield Oliver's *The French Dispute in Madagascar* (London, 1886), for a British account.

29. W. Edwards, *British Foreign Policy 1815–1933* (London, 1934), p. 162; and Parker T. Moon, *Imperialism in World Politics* (New York: The Macmillan Company, 1926), p. 134.

30. *Antananarivo Annual,* III, 135–36.

Chapter 3
The Lone Administrator

1. This policy did not include regular army personnel. All regulars were paid by Paris. The head tax as a factor contributing to the dilution of tribal economies in Madagascar has not been fully discussed anywhere, but some works have dealt with it. Of those, see Gayet, *La Circulation Monétaire et le Crédit à Madagascar* (Paris, 1923); Faublée, *Ethnographie de Madagascar* (Paris, 1946); and H. Guinaudeau, *Étude de la Situation Économique de la Grande Ile et des Moyens Susceptibles de l'Améliorer* (Tananarive, 1936).

2. Letter of April 27, 1898, *Lettres de Madagascar* (Paris, 1928), pp. 27–31.

3. Gallieni was *not* opposed to colonization. On the contrary, he strongly favored it, and statistics show that the number of settlers as well as exports increased considerably after the conquest. What he did oppose was the timing. *"Toute organisation doit suivre le pays dans son developpement naturel."* (Guillaume Grandidier, quoting Gallieni, in Dandouau and Chapus, *op. cit.,* p. 260.)

4. Letter of April 27, 1898, *loc. cit.*

5. See Gen. Lyautey, *Lettres du Sud de Madagascar* (Paris, 1935), and *Lettres du Tonkin et de Madagascar,* 2 vols. (Paris, 1920); also, André Lebon, *La Pacification de Madagascar* (Paris, 1928).

6. Letter of October 25, 1898, *loc. cit.*

7. Herbert I. Priestley, *France Overseas* (New York, 1938), p. 312.

8. *"Dès le 9 mars, 1902, un décret a réglementé (cette) institution pour la province centrale de l'Imerina. Un décret du 30 septembre, 1904, a autorisé le gouverneur général a étendre les dispositions de celui de 1902 à toutes les provinces de la colonie; ce qui a été realisé par une série d'arrêtés, échelonnés de 1904 à 1920."*

(Organisation Politique et Administrative des Colonies
[Brussels, 1936], p. 85.)
9. H. Deschamps and P. Chauvet, *Gallieni, Pacificateur*
(Paris, 1949), p. 357.

Chapter 4
THE MACHINE TAKES OVER

1. See his *Erreurs et Brutalités Coloniales* (Paris, 1927).
2. Priestley, *op. cit.,* p. 329.
3. *Destin d'Afrique* (Paris, 1930), p. 188.
4. Marcel Olivier, *Six Ans de Politique Sociale à Mada-*
gascar (Paris, 1931.)
5. RIIA, *The Colonial Problem* (London: Oxford University Press, 1937), p. 169.
6. Like the *Fokon'olona,* the EFD should be accorded a
much fuller discussion than possible within this brief
volume. There are, however, several excellent works
dealing with the two institutions. Among these, two
studies on the *Fokon'olona* should be singled out:
Pierre Delteil, *Le Fokon'olona* (Paris, 1930); and Fran-
cis Arbousset, *Le Fokon'olona à Madagascar* (Paris,
1950), the most recent work on the subject, which is
divided into three parts: "Le Fokon'olona sous la
Monarchie Merina (1787–1896)"; "Le Fokon'olona
dans la Législation Française (1896–1950)"; and "Le
Fokon'olona et la Jurisprudence des Tribuneaux Français." In addition, it contains the best single legal bibliography on Madagascar (sixty-seven authors and
ninety works), lists numerous official documents and
periodicals, and also has a short vocabulary of legal
and administrative terms in Malagasy. Arbousset comes
out for a revival of the *Fokon'olona* as an administrative, legal, and political institution functioning on two
levels—local and national. The best study dealing with
the EFD, its background, and its aim up to 1936, is
André Martin's *Les Délégations Économiques et Finan-*
cières de Madagascar (Paris, 1938), originally presented

as an LLB thesis at the University of Paris. This 250-page work consists of 5 parts, with 30 concise chapters and a very useful bibliography. Two studies of corollary institutions should also be mentioned. They are Guy Fenard's *Les Indigènes Fonctionnaires à Madagascar* (Paris, 1939, 269 pp.), and Olga Debousset's *L'Organisation Municipale à Madagascar* (Paris, 1942, 119 pp.). Fenard divides his work into two parts. The first deals with the replacement of the *Hova* functionaries by French officials and with the renewed employment of Malagasy (*Hova* in most cases) within the administration. The second part includes considerable data on reforms, management (*gestion*), and purely technical administrative problems. Olga Debousset's study deals with the *Fokon'olona* and with French *communes on* a comparative basis. Its main thesis is that the French *commune* is the center of "natural interests," whereas the *Fokon'olona* has become a legalistic and empty structure. She urges that if the *Fokon'olona* are to have a real and lasting value, they must be allowed to develop along lines similar to those of the *commune*.

7. E. Andriantsilaniarivo, "La Langue Malgache," *Madagascar*, p. 13.

8. See "Organisation de la Justice," *Madagascar, la Grande Ile* (Paris, 1939), p. 119.

9. See Deschamps, *The French Union* (Paris, 1956), p. 114.

10. "Mémoire en Défense Redigé par M. Ravoahangy, Député Détenu à la Prison Civile de Tananarive," *NED*, No. 714 (August 30, 1947), 17.

11. Decary, *op. cit.,* p. 49. The outlook implicit in his statement does not do full justice to Raymond Decary, one of the leading *malgachists*.

12. For example, those of November 6, 1930, February 11, 1931, and January 12, 1934 (standardization of produce prices); April 18, 1930 (*credit agricole*); September 18, 1930 (economic and financial delegations); November 15, 1930 (provincial divisions); December 26, 1930 (local indigenous personnel); May 23, 1932 (provincial

chiefs); July 17, 1933 (*conseils agricoles*); September 2, 1934 (*caisse agricole*); October 15, 1937 (central administrative region); October 30, 1935, December 22, 1935, and December 26, 1937 (commerce and duties); April 7, 1938 (labor regulations); October 28, 1938 (chambers of commerce); and December 21, 1938 (southern province status). The only significant law of that period is the 1938 decree on labor legislation. Madagascar was the first French colony to receive legislative authorization for labor unions. Joseph Ravoahangy was its principal animator and this was one of his most significant contributions to the evolution of Malagasy nationalism.

13. *Le Fokon'olona à Madagascar,* p. 256.

Chapter 5
THE "SPIRIT OF BRAZZAVILLE"

1. The decree of December 27, 1943, created a bureau known as Direction des Affaires Malgaches, as well as the Mixed Commission (*Journal Officiel de Madagascar,* January 1, 1944, p. 2). The latter body performed only one useful function prior to its abolition. It carried out an agricultural survey and made several recommendations eventually incorporated into the Plan Decennale (Tananarive, 1954). The equality principle was included only subsequently in the decree of January 22, 1944, which fixed the competence and the composition of the Mixed Commission (see *Journal Officiel de Madagascar* of January 29, 1944, p. 103).

2. *French Colonial Policy in Africa* (New York: Free France, Press and Information Service, September, 1944), p. 8.

3. By making all Malagasy citizens of both France and the French Union, the *loi Lamine Guéye* wiped out the last remnants of the *code indigénat*. For decrees of November 9, 1944, February 16, 1945, March 23, 1945, May 4, 1945, and September 1, 1945, see *Bulletin Hebdomaire des Colonies,* October 1, 1945.

4. "Propositions présentées par MM. Ravoahangy et Ra-

seta à l'Assemblée Nationale Constituante" (April 19, 1946) and "Programme du Comité Electoral de M. Raseta," *NED,* No. 714 (July 30, 1947). Also "Status du MDRM," *Journal Officiel,* No. 48 (February 25, 1947).

Chapter 6
THE REVOLT OF 1947

1. An interesting document on military operations against the rebel units—"Madagascar: La Situation Militaire à Madagascar au Jour le Jour, d'après les Communiqués de l'État-Major du Commandant Inter-armées, August 1–28, 1947"—can be found in the *Bulletin d'Information des Colonies,* September 22, 1947.

2. See John Gunther, *Inside Africa* (New York: Harper & Brothers, 1955), p. 601.

3. See, for example, Decary, "Madagascar," *La France de l'Océan Indien* (Paris, 1952), VIII, 56.

4. See P. Boiteau, *Contribution à l'Histoire de la Nation Malgache* (Paris, 1958), p. 224. The great weakness of Boiteau's volume is that it sees every aspect of life through heavily colored Marxist glasses, but it contains facts that are seldom, if ever, mentioned in most of the "orthodox" literature. Of particular use are his economic chapters.

5. Exports fell from an average of 250,000 metric tons a year to 140,000 in 1940, 112,000 in 1941, 28,000 in 1942, 73,000 in 1943, and 132,000 in 1944. Imports declined from a yearly average of 150,000 metric tons to 64,000 in 1940, 45,000 in 1941, 11,000 in 1942, 36,000 in 1943, and 62,000 in 1944. For a description of economic conditions in Madagascar between 1940 and 1944, see *Banque de Madagascar, Procès-verbal, Rapport du Conseil d'Administration,* Budget of December 31, 1940 (Paris, 1941), pp. 5–8; Budget of December 31, 1941 (Paris, 1942), pp. 3–4; Budget of May 11, 1943 (Paris, 1943), pp. 6–12; *Assemblée Général Ordinaire,* September 29, 1944, pp. 5–6, and September 28, 1945, pp. 5–15. The Bank's 1947–48 reports throw

some additional light on the economic repercussions of the revolt.

6. There is no extensive or significant literature on the 1940–43 period. Fragmentary reports can be obtained from A. Annet, *Aux Heures Troublées de l'Afrique Française, 1939–1943* (Paris, 1951); Charles de Gaulle, *Call to Honor* (New York: Simon and Schuster, 1955), pp. 237–43; "Les Réalisations de la France Combattante à Madagascar et à la Réunion," *NED*, No. 25 (February 27, 1945); and "Eclipse de Madagascar-Ce Que Fut 'Vichy' à Madagascar," *Revue de Madagascar*, January, 1945, pp. 10–17.

7. "Discours Prononcé par le Gouverneur Général de Madagascar à l'Occasion de la Première Session de l'Assemblée Representative, 19 Avril, 1947," *NED*, No. 713 (August 29, 1947), p. 10.

8. Mannoni's work has been translated into English by Pamela Powesland and published under the title *Prospero and Caliban, A Study of the Psychology of Colonization* (New York: Frederick A. Praeger, 1956).

9. Joseph Ravoahangy, "Mémoire en Défense," *NED*, No. 714 (August 30, 1947), p. 20.

10. "Discours Prononcés par le Gouverneur Général," *op. cit.*, pp. 10–11.

11. "Statement by the Minister for France Overseas, M. Moutet," *NED*, No. 713 (August 29, 1947), p. 16.

12. *Ibid.*

13. Remarks by Rabeantoandro, as quoted by Jacques Rabemananjara, *NED*, No. 714 (August 30, 1947), p. 10.

14. *Marchés Tropicaux du Monde*, No. 648 (April 12, 1958), p. 1005.

15. Preface to Chevalier. For further literature concerning the revolt and its aftermath, see H. Benazet, *L'Afrique Française en Danger* (Paris, 1947); Henry Casseville, *L'Ile Ensanglantée* (Paris, 1948); Olivier Hatzfield, *Madagascar* (Paris, 1951); Pierre Stibbe, *Justice pour les Malgaches* (Paris, 1954); and "L'Insurrection Malgache," *Bulletin des Missions* (Bruges), XXIV (1950).

Chapter 7
REFLECTIONS IN THE ECONOMY

1. "Le Marche de l'Emploi à Madagascar en 1956," *Bulletin de Madagascar*, No. 130 (March, 1957), 243.
2. *Renseignements Relatifs aux Territoires Non-autonomes. Résumé et Analyse des Renseignements Communiqués en Vertu de l'Article 73-e de la Charte.* Rapport du Secrétaire Général: Madagascar, Doc. A/4084/Add. 2, February 26, 1959, p. 26.
3. *Ibid.*, p. 7.

Crop	Type	1948	1953	1956
		(Area in hectares)		
Rice	consumer	567,000	697,300	738,000
Corn	"	82,000	83,000	69,000
Beans	"	28,000	36,300	54,500
Peas	"	18,000	13,700	12,500
Potatoes	"	28,000	21,700	23,000
Cassava	mixed	86,000	209,000	179,000
Yams	consumer	76,000	110,000	105,000
Peanuts	"	13,000	27,800	36,000
Sugar cane	cash	12,000	14,100	17,300
Coffee	"	93,000	125,000	176,000
Cloves	"	20,000	26,000	33,000
Vanilla	"	2,400	2,700	3,800
Sisal	"	19,300	15,200	12,800
Total		1,054,700	1,381,800	1,459,900

4. For a concise statement on the climatic conditions in the north, south, west, and the central plateau, see L. Dudley Stamps, *op. cit.*, p. 509. As in other "underdeveloped" areas, a population increase of several hundred thousand is not in itself capable of alleviating the problem of manpower shortage, while, on the other hand, consumption goes up considerably.

5. See *Marchés Tropicaux du Monde,* Special No. 626 (November 9, 1957), 2663–69, particularly map on page 2664.

6. The third stage (1957–60) added another 18 billion francs, to be spent primarily in the agricultural sector and the social sector. The FIDES allotment for Madagascar in 1958–59 amounted to 4.633 billion francs and can be favorably compared with the total (1958–59) allotment for all of former AEF, or 6.342 billion francs. It is also somewhat larger than the 1958–59 allotment for the Cameroons of 4.584 billion francs. (See *Marchés Tropicaux du Monde,* No. 677 [August 23, 1958].)

7. Chevalier, *op. cit.,* pp. 179–80.

8. The term "underdeveloped" does apply to Madagascar, but it needs clarification, for it is being used with less and less meaning. For example, it is being applied to countries like Egypt, which, while not rich in natural resources, are anything but underdeveloped. (See Charles Issawi's *Egypt at Mid-Century* [London, 1954], and Doreen Warriner's *Land Reform and Development in the Middle East* [London, 1957], pp. 10–54.) Madagascar's natural wealth is not well researched as yet, and it may be moderately wealthy or quite rich in what its subsoil has to offer. It is, however, definitely underdeveloped agriculturally (less than one third of the cultivable land is cropped, and not all of it efficiently), and agriculture is the main pillar of its economy.

9. H. Perrier de la Bathie, "Des Sols de Madagascar et des Plantes qui en Indiquent la Valeur," *Revue de Botanique Appliquée et d'Agriculture Tropicale,* XIV, Nos. 156, 157 (1934), 765–79. An English agricultural expert brought to Madagascar recently has revised the Bathie estimate upward to 10 million hectares.

10. The trade-union movement split into two groups: the non-Communist CFTC and the Communist-controlled FISEMA (former CGT for Madagascar). In 1956, trade-union membership amounted to 40,000, of which 60

per cent belonged to the CFTC. For a concise review, see *Bulletin de Madagascar*, No. 135 (August, 1957), pp. 673–74; *l'Économie*, No. 615 (December 19, 1957); and *Marchés Tropicaux du Monde*, No. 658 (June 21, 1958).

Chapter 8
THE POLITICS OF INDEPENDENCE

1. "Interrogatoire de M. Rabemananjara," *NED*, No. 714 (August 30, 1947), p. 13.
2. See Robert Boudry, "Décolonisation à Madagascar?" *La Pensée, Revue de Rationalisme Moderne*, No. 78 (March–April, 1958), pp. 58–59. In orientation, the article parallels Pierre Boiteau's *Contribution to Malagasy History*.
3. *"Le premier acte du nouveau maire de Tananarive fut d'aller saluer les cendres d'Andrianampoinimerina, qui, le premier formula le principe de l'unité malgache."* (Boudry, *op. cit.*, p. 60.)
4. See "Deux Prises de Position Malgaches," *Le Monde*, August 3, 1957, for the main outline of the statement.
5. See "C'est avec Raison que l'Assemblée Nationale a Exclu des Activités Politiques Jusqu'en 1963, les Parlamentaires Malgaches Responsables de la Rébellion," *Marchés Tropicaux du Monde*, No. 648 (April 12, 1948), pp. 1005–6.
6. For a full text of the following *loi cadre* provisions applicable to Madagascar, consult "Réformes Outre-Mer," *Journal Officiel*, No. 1100 (September, 1957): Décret No. 57–462 of April 4, 1957 (Articles 1–17, pp. 75–80); Décret No. 57–463 of April 4, 1957 (Articles 1–70, pp. 81–99); Décret No. 57–464 of April 4, 1957 (Articles 1–68, pp. 101–18); Décret No. 57–816 of July 22, 1957 (Articles 1–11, pp. 119–21).
7. For elections for March 31, 1957, and parties listed, see *Bulletin Quotidien d'Outre Mer*, Agence France Press ("Composition of Territorial Assemblies in Black Africa and Madagascar"), April 15, 1957. See also "Les

Partis Politiques à Madagascar," *Marchés Tropicaux
du Monde,* No. 746 (February 27, 1960).

8. "From Bandung to Cairo," *International Affairs* (Moscow), No. 2 (February, 1958), p. 55. Razhaofera is one of the three founders of the literary magazine *Antso* (Appeal), which first appeared in 1938. His legal-political claim to being the "representative of Madagascar" was as questionable at the time as his right to being a representative Malagasy intellectual was legitimate.

9. *Marchés Tropicaux du Monde,* No. 675 (October 18, 1958), p. 2559.

10. *Marchés Tropicaux du Monde,* No. 678 (November 8, 1958), p. 2712.

11. See *ACCORDS Signés ou Paraphés le 2 avril 1960 entre le Gouvernement de la République Française et le Gouvernement de la République Malgache* (New York: Press and Information Bureau, The French Embassy, 1960).

12. See "Constitution du 29 Avril 1959 de la République Malgache," *Journal Officiel de Madagascar, No. 41* (April 29, 1959).

Conclusion

1. The system of communes has been strengthened by a new revision of May 29, 1959. There are at present 20 urban *communes de plein exercise;* 6 urban *communes de moyen exercise;* and 739 *communes rurales,* of which 67 are in the provinces of Diégo-Suarez, 197 in Fianarantsao, 114 in Majunga, 117 in Tamtave, 135 in Tananarive, and 109 in Tuléar. The Preamble to the Malagasy Constitution is almost exclusively devoted to individual rights. It reflects the experiences under centralism. For an outline of Tsiranana's outlook and policies, see his *Discours* (Tananarive, 1959). For the role of the *communes* in recent elections, consult *October 11, 1959, Elections in Madagascar,* available at the French Embassy, Press and Information Division, New York.

Selected Bibliography

Part One

ADRIAMANJATO, RICHARD. *Le Tsiny et le Tody dans la Pensée Malgache*. Paris, 1957.

ANICAN, G. "La Vie des Betsiléo à Madagascar," *Bulletin du Comité des Travaux Historiques et Scientifiques* (Paris), 1955, pp. 1–75.

ARBOUSSET, FRANÇOIS. *Le Fokon'olona à Madagascar*. Paris, 1950.

BAUDIN, E. "Chez les Sakalaves," *Revue de Madagascar*, October, 1937, pp. 7–40.

BERTHIER, HUGHES. *Notes et Impressions sur les Moeurs et Coutumes du Peuple Malgache*. Tananarive, 1933.

Bulletin de Madagascar. 1923, pp. 11–34, 205–32; 1925, pp. 5–47.

CHAMLA, MARIE-CLAUDE. *Recherches Anthropologiques sur l'Origine des Malgaches*. Paris, 1958.

CONDAMINAS, G. *Fokon'olona et Communautés Rurales en Imerina*. Paris, 1960.

COTTE, VINCENT. *Regardons Vivre une Tribu Malgache: Les Betsimisaraka*. Paris, 1947.

DANDOUAU, A. *Contes Populaires des Sakalava et Tsimihety*. Paris, 1922.

DECARY, RAYMOND. *Les Antandroy*. 2 vols. Paris, 1930–33.

———. *Moeurs et Coutumes des Malgaches*. Paris, 1951.

DESCHAMPS, HUBERT. *Les Anteisaka*. Tananarive, 1936.

———. *Les Migrations Intérieures à Madagascar*. Paris, 1959.

————. *Histoire de Madagascar* (2d ed.). Paris, 1961. Pp. 1–263.

———— and VIANES, SUZANNE. *Les Malgaches du Sud-Est.* Paris, 1959.

DUBOIS, HENRY. *Monographie des Betsiléos.* Paris, 1938.

FAUBLÉE, JACQUES. *Ethnographie de Madagascar.* Paris, 1946.

————. *La Cohésion des Sociétés Bara.* Paris, 1953.

FERRAND, GABRIEL. "Madagascar," *Encyclopedie de l'Islam.* Paris, 1936. Vol. III.

FRERE, SUZANNE. *Panorama de l'Androy.* Paris, 1958.

GRANDIDIER, ALFRED and GUILLAUME. *Ethnographie de Madagascar.* 5 vols. Paris, 1908–17.

LINTON, RALPH. *The Tanala: A Hill Tribe of Madagascar.* ("Field Museum of Natural History Anthropological Series," Publication No. 317, XXII.) Chicago, 1933.

LONGUEFOSSE, M. "L'Antsihanaka. Région du Lac Alaotra à Madagascar," *Bulletin de Madagascar,* 1922, p. 233–48; 1923, pp. 111–34, 205–32; 1925, pp. 5–47.

MAGNES, E. "Essai sur les Institutions et la Coutume des Tsimihety," *Revue de Madagascar,* October, 1953.

MATTEI, L. "Les Tsimihety," *Bulletin Académie Malgache,* XXI (1938), 131–96.

MICHEL, LÉON. *Moeurs et Coutumes Bara.* Tananarive, 1957.

MOLET, LOUIS. *Le Bain Royal à Madagascar.* Paris, 1956.

————. *Démographie de l'Ankaizinana.* Tananarive, 1957.

ROBEQUAIN, CHARLES. *Madagascar et les Bases Dispersées de l'Union Française.* Paris, 1958.

Part Two

ATTULY, ROBERT. *Le Droit Pénal à Madagascar.* Paris, 1924.

AUGAGNEUR, VICTOR. *Erreurs et Brutalités Coloniales.* Paris, 1927.

BENAZET, HENRY. *L'Afrique Française en Danger.* Paris, 1947.

CAILLET, EMILE. *Essai sur la Psychologie Hova.* Paris, 1924.

CHAILEY-BERT, J. *Dix Ans de Politique Coloniale.* Paris, 1902.

CHERRIER, R. *La Législation Concernant le Travail Indigène à Madagascar.* Paris, 1932.

DE CASSEVILLE, HENRY. *L'Ile Ensanglantée.* Paris, 1948.

DESCHAMPS, HUBERT. *Madagascar* (2d ed.). Paris, 1951.

GARBIT, HUGHES. *L'Effort de Madagascar Pendant la Guerre.* Paris, 1919.

GHEUSI, PIERRE B. *Gallieni et Madagascar.* Paris, 1931.

GRANDIDIER, GUILLAUME. *Gallieni.* Paris, 1931.

GUINAUDEAU, H. *Étude de la Situation Économique de la Grande Ile et Moyens Susceptibles de l'Ameliorer.* Tananarive, 1936.

HATZFIELD, OLIVER. *Madagascar.* Paris, 1951.

"Insurrection Malgache," *Bulletin Missions Abbaye Saint-Andre-les-Bruges,* XXIV (1950).

JULIEN, GUSTAVE. *Madagascar et se Dépendances.* Paris, 1930.

KENT, RAYMOND K. "The Malagasy Republic," *The Educated African,* ed. HELEN KITCHEN. New York: Frederick A. Praeger, 1962.

LEBEL, CHARLES. *Standardisation à Madagascar,* Paris, 1937.

LEBLOND, MARIUS-ARY. *Madagascar, Création Française.* Paris, 1934.

LEBON, ANDRÉ. *La Pacification de Madagascar.* Paris, 1928.

MANNONI, DOMINIQUE-O. "L'Enseignement," *Madagascar, Encyclopedie Coloniale.* Paris, 1947.

OLIVIER, MARCEL. *Six Ans de la Politique Sociale à Madagascar.* Paris, 1931.

PRUNIERES, ANDRÉ. *Madagascar et la Crise.* Paris, 1936.

RABEMANANJARA, RAYMOND W. *Madagascar sous la Renovation Malgache.* Paris, 1953.

RENEL, CHARLES. *Le Décivilisé.* Paris, 1923.

ROBINSON, KENNETH. "French Africa and French Union," *Africa Today* (Baltimore, 1955).

RUSILLON, HENRY. *Un Petit Continent, Madagascar.* Paris, 1933.

You, André. *Madagascar, Colonie Française, 1896–1930.* Paris, 1931.

Part Three

Bargues, Robert. *Discours.* Tananarive, 1951.

Boudry, Robert. " 'Decolonisation' à Madagascar?" *La Pensée,* No. 78 (March–April, 1958), pp. 43–65.

Brun-Keris, George. "Madagascar à l'Heure de la Loi-Cadre," *Marchés Tropicaux du Monde,* No. 626 (November 9, 1957), pp. 2610–15.

Bulletin de L'Association pour l'Étude des Problemes de l'Union Française:
"La Situation Politique à Madagascar," No. 85 (February, 1955).
"Nationalisme et Independance à Madagascar," No. 23 (April, 1958).

Bulletin de Madagascar:
" 'Livre de Raison' de Madagascar, 1946–1956," Nos. 135–37 (August–October, 1957).
"Bilan de 1957," No. 139 (December, 1957), pp. 1017–70.
"Évolution de l'Économie Malgache en 1958," No. 162 (November, 1959), pp. 945–83.
"August–November, 1956," Nos. 123–26, pp. 694–713, 785–802, 854–88, 954–68.

Démocratie Nouvelle, ed. Jacques Duclos. No. 5 (May, 1958); No. 7 (July, 1958).

Deschamps, Hubert. *The French Union.* Paris, 1956.

———. *Histoire de Madagascar.* (2d ed.). Paris, 1961, pp. 264–316.

Information Économique, Financière, Juridique de Madagascar. No. 1 (January–February, 1957); No. 3 (May–June, 1957).

Isnard, Hildebert. *Madagascar.* Paris, 1955.

L'Économie. Supplement, November 29, 1951; No. 472 (December 17, 1954); No. 534 (April 5, 1956); No. 615 (December 12, 1957).

L'Esprit. XVI (February, 1948). Special issue on Madagascar.

L'Exportateur. December 1, 1951. Special issue.

L'Information. October 5, 1954.

La Documentation Française, Notes et Études Documentaires. Nos. 1799; 1800; 1801; 1875; 1897.

"Madagascar, Republique Soeur," *Le Monde,* August 11, 12, 13, 1959.

Marchés Tropicaux du Monde. Nos. 600–634 (1957); Nos. 648, 652, 675, 678 (1958).

MINISTÈRE DE FOM. *Données Numériques sur l'Union Française.* Paris, 1956.

Problèmes Économiques. No. 138 (August 22, 1950).

RABEMANANJARA, JACQUES. *Nationalisme et Problèmes Malgaches* (Paris, 1958).

Résonances. 4e Trimestre, 1952. Special issue on Madagascar.

RIVIERE, J. *La Situation Économique et Financière.* Tananarive, 1956.

SOUCADAUX, ANDRÉ. *Discours* (Tananarive), April, 1956.

STIBBE, PIERRE. *Justice Pour les Malgaches.* Paris, 1954.

TSIRANANA, PHILIBERT. *Discours* (Tananarive), October, 1959.

Index